Improve Your PRESENTATION SKILLS

By
Ishita Bhown

Published by:

F-2/16, Ansari Road, Daryaganj, New Delhi-110002
011-23240026, 011-23240027 • *Fax:* 011-23240028
Email: info@vspublishers.com • *Website:* www.vspublishers.com

Regional Offi ce : Hyderabad
5-1-707/1, Brij Bhawan (Beside Central Bank of India Lane)
Bank Street, Koti, Hyderabad - 500 095
040-24737290
E-mail: vspublishershyd@gmail.com

Branch Offi ce : Mumbai
Godown # 34 at The Model Co-Operative Housing, Society Ltd.,
"Sahakar Niwas", Ground Floor, Next to Sobo Central, Mumbai - 400 034
022-23510736
E-mail vspublishersmum@gmail.com

Follow us on:

All books available at **www.vspublishers.com**

© **Copyright:** V&S PUBLISHERS
ISBN 978-93-813841-0-7
Edition 2014

The Copyright of this book, as well as all matter contained herein (including illustrations) rests with the Publisher. No person shall copy the name of the book, its title design, matter and illustrations in any form and in any language, totally or partially or in any form. Anybody doing so shall face legal action and will be responsible for damages.

Printed at : Param Offseters Okhla New Delhi-110020

Publisher's Note

The ability of a person to convince other people about his unique and novel idea through his/her speaking abilities, knowledge of the subject and computer skills, i.e., the PowerPoint Presentations which have almost become a part and parcel of everyone's life is together called as **Presentation Skills.**

In today's world, students studying in schools and colleges as well as people working in various Government offices and MNCs face a tough competition. It is not always easy to convey all the knowledge one has in an effective way to the audience. Sometimes, it is important to filter out the salient aspects and highlight them in a simpler language, which can be easily understood by the listeners. One should be capable of conveying the information or one's idea in an effective manner. *Positioning yourself and your ideas in a consistently positive and professional manner helps in making a professional impression, and most presentations consist of facts or logical arguments put into a sequence along with one's own analysis and speaking abilities.*

The book deals with all the above mentioned ways and methods to *improve and enhance the Presentation Skills of a person, whether, he or she is a student, a professional, an employee, a businessman, a bureaucrat or a housewife.*

Basically, Successive and Persuasive Presentations begin with the collection of raw information, opinions are added to make it effective, colours are added with imagery to make it interesting, and such presentations create long lasting impressions on the minds of the listeners. It also improvises your own personality as a Speaker and helps to connect a chord with the Audience, which is the actual aim of the book.

Hope the book serves its purpose well by transforming You into a Successful and Efficient Speaker/Presenter!

Contents

Chapter : 1
Why Do You Need This Book? 7

Chapter : 2
The Five Steps of a Successful Presentation 13

Chapter : 3
Find It! 19

Chapter : 4
Organise It 36

Chapter : 5
Tailor It 68

Chapter : 6
Remember and Rehearse 87

Chapter : 7
Content Delivery 97

Chapter : 8
Visual Aids 111

Chapter : 9
A-Z of Presentation Skills 117

Chapter

A person can have the greatest idea in the world, completely different and novel, but if that person can't convince enough other people, it doesn't matter.

Case Study: 1

Suyash works as an analyst in one of the famous IT consulting companies. He is known among his colleagues as the most sincere and promising employee and is greatly revered for his dedication towards work. His job is to write reports to support decision making processes. His work profile includes almost no contact with the clients. He has to make the reports and be very good at his analytics. One of the firm's client decided that it was time for them to see the big picture and have a direct discussion before giving the assignment to that company. The client was very important to the company. Because of his good image and command over the reports, Suyash was an obvious choice for the scheduled presentation. He spoke for about 30 minutes and it all went very well, or at least he thought so. Unfortunately, it turned out that the client didn't quite share his views. The clients were not convinced about the utility of the report, the findings that were presented, and had almost decided on giving the assignment to some other company.

As a last attempt, Suyash's assistant, who had been closely working on the report gave it a hurried try and improvised another presentation on the spot, one which, happily, did the job. The client calmed down, and gave him another chance to 'come prepared' for another presentation. The assistant managed to buy some more time and save the situation, but this left Suyash wondering .He introspected where he had gone wrong.

Analysis:

Such situations are very common in daily life, especially in work environments. In today's competitive era, good information, great ideas or the best proposal only gets you half way. To be a successful professional presenter, you need to capture your audience and take them on your journey using effective presentations, and for this, you require effective presentation skills.

Case Study: 2

Radhika, who was a final year student at one of the reputed engineering colleges was excited to be nominated for her summer training at IIT, Delhi. The 2-month training gave her a chance to explore newer dimensions towards her academic subjects. Her sincerity and intelligence gave her an opportunity to be closely associated with a research project undertaken by the senior professors. This gave her a chance to learn about the latest developments in science and technology, the knowledge, which most of her peers had failed to gain. After the completion of training, when she returned to her own college, she was requested by the teachers and the Dean to share the knowledge and the experiences with her juniors. She happily accepted the chance, and prepared a presentation covering all the aspects of the project, she had undertaken. She made sure to include all the details that she knew. Radhika introduced the newer concepts that she had learnt, and also discussed them in detail with proper examples and the way they were implemented in the upcoming project. With the kind of detailing that she had done, she was confident to win appreciation. But, at the end of her one hour presentation, she was not very satisfied with the kind of feedback given by her Dean. The audience could not understand most of the technical terms, she had used. She was shocked and decided to introspect about the mistake she (had) possibly committed.

Analysis:

Such situations are often faced in schools and colleges. It is not always easy to convey all your knowledge in an effective way to the audience. Sometimes, it is important to filter out the salient aspects and highlight them in a simpler language, which is understood by the listeners. Both the case studies above, clearly tell that it is not sufficient to have knowledge. One should be capable of conveying the information in an effective manner. Positioning yourself and your ideas in a consistently positive and professional manner helps in making a professional impression — *the first time and every time.*

Most presentations consist of facts or logical arguments put into a sequence. The problem is that this sequence often makes no sense. It is dull. It is difficult to follow. It does not answer to the obvious question that comes to the audience- "So what?" The audience is forced to follow the chain of thoughts without understanding where it is leading us and why. Presenters tend to put a lot of dots on the board without really connecting them. The presenter at times, may get lost in his/her own collection of facts and may end up repeating the same points or even diverting from the topic. They forget what to say next. How can we expect people to listen to any story, when the storyteller is confused and does not deliver in an interesting manner. *Raw information is logical, but being logical is not sufficient to capture anyone's attention for too long.*

> **TIP:** *Persuasive presentations begin with the collection of raw information, opinions are added to make it effective, colours are added with imagery to make it interesting, and such presentations create long lasting impressions on the minds of the listeners. It also improvises your own personality as a Speaker.*

Persuasive presentations help to connect a chord with the audience and to tickle their minds. The more of the mind you tickle, the more retention and motivation you reap. A successful presentation is more like telling a factual story, which is much easier to create. You don't need to make up facts. The facts are already there. All you need to do is to select the right facts and put them in a sequence. A good speaker has the skills of integrating the relevant facts and conveying them in 'an easy to remember way'. You must always remember that your time is limited, and you have to speak about some topics and leave some others out.

Where are Presentation Skills Needed?

Presentations are an extremely complex and expensive form of human communication. The interaction is relatively short but the combined time of all the people involved costs a lot.

Despite their complexities and costs, people prefer presentations in daily life, that's simply because they are also sometimes *tremendously impactful. Also, sometimes, there's a lot at stake.*

Presentations are useful not just in offices, businesses, corporates etc., but also form an integral part in educational institutes, social life and day to day interactions. Almost any kind of activity involves some degree of presentation skills. Sharing your knowledge among the peers, communicating the purpose and content of any trainings or projects made during the school or college days, guiding a new colleague through the basic office procedures, reporting back to a departmental meeting, any kind of sales call (by telephone or face-to-face), or giving the members of the board an overview of a new product, highlighting the positives of your products – in each situation, you will be giving a presentation.

"Presentations have become the *de facto* communication tool," writes *presentation design Guru, Nancy Duarte*. Companies are started, products are launched, and climate systems are saved — possibly based on the quality of presentations. Ideas, endeavours, and even careers can be cut short due to ineffective communication.

People give *presentations before commencing expensive projects and after finishing them.* It makes sense to conduct extensive preparations in these cases, and there's almost no limit on how deep and wide you can go. Good presentations need *rehearsals, rearrangement of thoughts, expressions in the form of slides,* and you need *intensive research for new arguments* in support of the point.

Unfortunately, out of the millions of presentations delivered each day, only a small percentage is delivered well. Improperly laid presentations are troublesome for both-the speaker and the audience. The audience feels bored and disinterested, while the presenter feels bad about not being able to convey his/

her ideas. There are *some basic principles that if followed will turn a poor presentation into a great one.* There's no mystery about creating and delivering effective presentations – you just need to find out how to do it right. *We're talking about a skill, and like any other skill, it can be learnt.* It is no rocket science.

People frequently think that presentations are about *delivery*, about *acting skills*, and about *how you say, what you have to say*. In the end, these aspects are what we see and hear, but are only a part of the presentation skills. People also think that presentations are mostly about slides, which depict the content in the written form. People spend lots of time designing the right slides and making them, so that they can work with or without the actual presenter.

Apart from slides, focus is also needed on the structure and argumentation, which is an important contributor. It has to do with what you say rather than how you say it.

This part requires storytelling, script and speech writing skills, and a deep knowledge of the content. All these skills combine together to assist a person is giving successful presentations, which once practised are useful in all sorts of official requirements.

It's Not What You Say, It's How You Say It....

According to one of the best-known myths in the presentation business, Communication happens at three levels:

- ✓ Visual – 55% (Body Language)
- ✓ Vocal – 38% (Voice Tone)
- ✓ Verbal – 7% (Words)

By far, *visual communication is the most powerful of the three types.*

Similar information regularly appears in any number of locations. Going by this piece of information, one may imagine that as long as one gets his/her body language right, the words don't really matter. Often people jump to the conclusion, that only good body language and confidence can render good presentations and this assumption runs the risk of producing a very poor presentation. Visual communication holds around 55% impact in the overall communication, *yet the content and the verbal parts cannot totally be neglected.*

However, there are certain questions; we need to answer for ourselves, before committing to presentations.

Ever Wondered!

Have you ever wondered how well do you know your own voice? Is it deep and gruff, about average or a little high pitched? Do you speak quickly, slowly or at a medium pace? Do you have an extensive range of tones and inflections which make your voice interesting to listen to, or (be honest) does your voice tend to become rather monotonous if you have to speak continuously for more than four to five minutes?

In the UK and the USA, a person who speaks slowly and in a lower-than-average tone is widely perceived as being powerful and credible. Someone with a faster, higher-toned voice will be seen as enthusiastic but lightweight and positively untrustworthy.

How will your speech be perceived among the audience, and will it leave the desired effect? There are many similar concerns that need our attention, and that should be honestly considered before speaking on the stage. Similarly, your choice of words directly influence the audience's attention. At times, the words that are fun, tangible and uncommon in most professional dealings maybe, a welcome change in your presentations and can assist in bringing smiles among the listeners.

How to choose the words which help in connecting a chord with the audience and what about your body language? Did you know that a person whose gestures are few and far between is seen as being powerful, deliberate and intelligent? The sort of person who makes frequent, expansive gestures may be seen as frivolous. How to work upon a presentation, that maintains a proper balance and can fulfill the audience's needs?

Customers may be willing to accept higher prices if they also get the preferential status or better quality. Conversely, they may be willing to accept lower quality – as long as it is still within certain tolerances and as long as they get a better base price and bigger discounts. The teachers and professors should be convinced that you have actually worked hard upon the concept, and you are aware of the in detailed knowledge of the concerned topic. Your presentation should convey that you have not merely mugged up the things.

But whatever it is that you are offering as a differentiator, your audience must know about it. They must still be convinced that what *you* are offering, at *your* prices, etc is the best fit for *their* requirements. In practice, the only way you can really differentiate yourself is by making the most *effective sales pitch – the most impressive presentation.*

This book deals with some very simple steps that help in developing effective presentation skills. It covers three major topics concerned with presentations: **Structure, Content (Slides) and Delivery.**

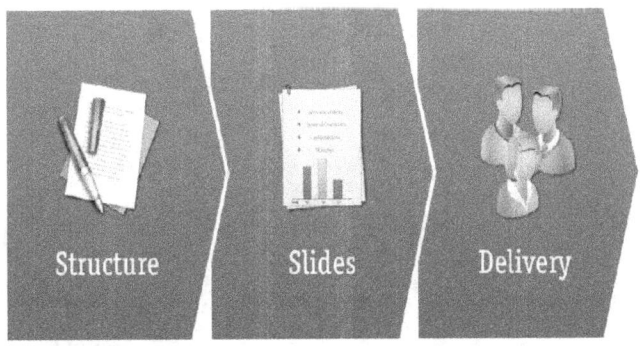

It includes the basics of storytelling, how the narrative part of presentation should be constructed and connected to create a sequence which leads the audience from the *established status quo* through the conflict to the *resolution* and *new balance*.

It also deals with *slides*, which serve *four major goals, such as: to remind, to impress, to explain,* and *to prove.* The importance of *aesthetic design, body language, the language of communication* and the other significant things to focus on during a live presentation will be explained in detail in the chapters that follow ahead.

Chapter 2

Once you have been tasked with preparing a presentation, after the initial research, you decide to go ahead with it. You should discover the purpose or a list of objectives that you need to cater, and then begins the actual work towards giving shape to your thoughts, and voice to your ideas. Before focussing on the mechanics of the slides, its aesthetics, the visuals, clip

Once you are clear with the content, start focussing on the delivery of the content in an interesting manner that can hold the attention of the audience.

The Five Salient Steps to Develop Presentations:

There are five basic steps that help in developing effective presentations, which maybe used in all situations, such as: offices, product launches, client visits, etc., The steps sometimes seem overcomplicated when in fact, after due practice, can be moved through fairly quickly. The amount of time you spend on each step will reflect the importance of the presentation. The more important the step, the more time needs to be spent on the preparations.

1. Find It
2. Organise It
3. Tailor It
4. Remember It
5. Deliver It

1. Find It

This first section is about gathering all your information into one place, going through it and understanding what's relevant and what's not. To get a chance for presentation is a unique experience – filled with multiple emotions- fear, gratification, nervousness and an immense sense of responsibility to make it an effective one.

However, it is not advised to grab the opportunity, without properly evaluating it. One should be cent percent sure of his/her ability to do the best before taking up the challenge. Try to find out more details about the event and then set your presentation points accordingly. Gather as much information about the audience as is possible, so that you can know about the expectation level of the deliverables. Basically, it is advised to collect information on the following heads and work carefully on each on them:

The context: It refers to the information about why you are presenting. what is the situation, the medium, the subject, the audience and the objective of your presentation. Work upon each of these details to set a purpose of the presentation. Once you are clear on it, it will be easier for you to sort out the relevant details to be included.

Your credibility: It is mostly concerned with self-evaluation. You need to understand where you sit in the eyes of your audience. Have you met them before, do they have any preconceptions about you, are you well regarded, or do you have some ground to make up? Based on this analysis, you'll be able to determine where you sit with your "who" factor. It's up to you to maintain, build, or repair your credibility.

Filters and motivation: It involves detailed insights into your audience and what motivates them. Understand the communication filters and expectations of your audience and think about how you are going to tailor your message by analysing the audience's characteristics and subsequent communication preferences.

Evidence: Try to gather all the types of information that is going to backup the content of your presentation. Include as many types of relevant evidences that you can and make it persuasive. Facts, personal experiences, examples, analogies, all may be suitably included and cited at the correct places.

The detailed information about finding all the information to make a meaningful presentation is explained in detail in Chapter-3.

2. Organise It:

When preparing a presentation, many people begin with structure, saying all that they know about their topic in the allotted time. With the "Find It" step of the presentation, the process of structuring your presentation becomes easier as you only use the information that you know will help you achieve your objective.

Using a structure that is easy to follow will help the audience in retaining the information presented.

At this stage, you need to review the content against your objective. Are you on track or do you need to add or remove information? The selection of content greatly depends upon the length of your presentation. Suppose, you just have 5 minutes to convey your message-then it becomes mandatory to directly speak about the relevant points only. Suppose the length of the presentation is increased, then you need proper planning, and a roadmap is preferred. It is advisable to convey the presentation outline to the audience, so that they can prepare themselves accordingly.

Case Study:

Jai, who was a well learned mathematician, was asked to share some tips with the students on Keshavanath School. He happily accepted to give a session that would cover all the significant chapters and topics of the curriculum. On the decided date, he was made to address a group of 60 students. When he entered the classroom, all the students gave him a blank look. It took him no time to realise that his audience was clueless about the purpose of the gathering. He gracefully introduced himself to the students, and told them about the agenda of the session. He had already divided the content in to various segments, separate modules for *Algebra*, *Trigonometry*, *Calculus* and so on. He clearly informed the students beforehand about the length of the session, and the various modules and their emphasis. He made sure to give some break after completion of each module. This eased the students, and they were now willing to pay attention to Jai. This way, by proper organisation of the content, Jai was able to give a successful presentation and leave a positive impact among the students.

Analysis:

A well-organised presentation can be absorbed with minimal mental strain. Bridging is the key. The content should be divided in to various reasonable modules, and should be road mapped with the help of arrows. To get the audience's attention throughout the session, they should be kept aware about the direction in which the session is progressing. The outline should be made clear and time constraints should be kept in mind. If the audience is unaware of the benefits, or the agenda of your presentation, they will never be able to co-relate the things. Whether your presentation is short or long, you need to ensure, you have a clear *beginning, middle and end*. This communication fundamental will hold you in good stead when organising your presentation.

In addition, begin with the end in mind so that you don't move away from the topic, as you put all your information together.

3. Tailor It:

After the completion of 'Find It' and 'Organise It' phase, the content is almost finalised. We now need to refine your work and style it. We are going to do this by doing three things; checking for relevance, choosing your words carefully and being articulate.

When tailoring your presentation, don't overlook the need to ruthlessly skip any information that is not relevant. Judge the audience, and choose the information that may be interesting to them.

After you have selected the content, then choose the method to convey it. Suppose, you have to use charts or graphs in the presentation, or simply make use of a white board to note down the important points, whatever is your chosen method, it is then needed to design the slides and make them look attractive.

Secondly, pay attention to the words you use. This is not a contest as to how clever you can be and how many different turns of phrase, you can use, but rather, how you can sparingly and tactfully use better expressions to explain your ideas. The words should be wisely chosen-It is advised to use the terms that are familiar with the audience. To make the session interesting, it is good to keep it interactive. Suppose, it's an informal gathering, then you can use the sense of humour to break the monotony, and after a light joke, the attention of the audience is returned to the session.

> **TIP:** *It is advised not to use many numbers and fill your presentation with facts and figures. You can use jingles or interesting phrases to make a positive impression.*

Try to involve the audience. The audience becomes best involved through their applause, laughter and response to any sort of call for action. You may ask the audience certain questions, and ask them to raise their hands in response, or follow some similar techniques to get their attention.

The main aim is to tailor the presentation in such a fashion, that the audience finds it interesting. You can freely use the visual aids, hand signals, interesting and catchy sentences, impressive slides or any other technique that you feel may do the trick. We need to explain our audience in the simplest and interesting manner. *If you can't explain it simply, you don't understand it well enough.*

4. Remember It:

Everyone has a different way of remembering what they have to say. Whatever technique you use, ensure that it is effective by rehearsing. If possible, record your presentation and play it back so that you can listen to how your audience will hear you. The best way to deliver a presentation is to use your own words. *A presentation is a sequence of thoughts;* if the thoughts are out of sequence, *the presentation won't make much sense.*

The way to remember a presentation is to use 'key phrases' and 'rehearse'. Before delivering any presentation, identify the crucial key phrases that are the most important parts of your presentation. *They need not be complete sentences, but even simple words may serve the purpose.*

Similarly, rehearsal plays the most important role in a presentation. Even the perfectly designed and tailored presentation may lose its significance, if the content is not properly delivered. *Rehearsal helps in removing the anxiety and provides the confidence.*

Practising is the best way to avoid the stage fear, and this assists in preparing an impressive presentation. It's true that a touch of anxiety makes for a better presentation, but too much anxiety leads to the opposite results. When you are overanxious about the presentation, the raw emotions that makes for a successful performance is replaced by a faltering, unstructured and disorganised speech. To manage the mix of all these emotions perfectly, the easiest way is to rehearse by speaking in front of the mirror, or even at the venue. Read the content again and again, and be comfortable with it. It is not needed to memorise all the sentences word by word, but you should be able to cover all the important points.

5. Deliver It:

The delivery of your presentation is what people typically find the most challenging. If you work on your strategy and content, your delivery will start to take care of itself. Your audience will forgive a few *ums* and *ah's* but they won't forgive the poor content. After carefully choosing your content, we need to smoothly flow from one point of the presentation to the another. When we speak, the audience does not have any idea about the slides, the headings or sub-headings, etc. It is the responsibility of the speaker to guide them through proper speech and clear organisation. Without proper flow of speech, the presentation will look confusing and disorganised.

If you want to effectively communicate with your audience, to influence, persuade or just create a good impression, you need to adapt your delivery style to match the expectations and communication needs of your audience.

This is about increasing the size of your delivery skill toolbox so that you can use the right tool for the job. This takes work and practice but the good news is your tool box is different from everyone else's. So your version of dynamic voice will be different to everyone else's, and your version of seriousness and intensity of the voice will also be different from everyone else's. Use facial expressions, eye contact, a firm and confident body language to get the audience's attention. Gestures, proper voice modulations, pitch variations, etc are all an integral part of your delivery skills.

> ***TIP:*** *Freely make use of the techniques like pause, repetition, emphasis, lists or asking questions to deliver your presentation in an interesting manner.*

When you have prepared your presentation well, revised and mastered its content, and have even rehearsed its proper delivery, which makes you confident about your performance on stage, it makes you feel ready to face the podium. But remember, there is another outstanding task, which forms a crucial aspect of your session. Prepare for a question and answer round. Whether it is an official meeting, or a presentation in educational institutes, or a sales pitch for business transaction, there is always a pool of questions in the audience's mind. Prepare well, and ask the audience if they have any doubts. The answers should be brief, logical and to the point, so that they satisfy the audience.

Chapter 3

We live in a world in which nobody knows how to do anything. In can put any individual on a winning edge. With so much information available on the internet, you need to be selective and careful about the content that should be marked as important.

To express yourself effectively is the need of the hour. We have to connect via phone conversations, written reports, e-mails, instant messaging, blogs, microblogs, and via just plain water cooler conversations -- some such forms of communication are used in routine conversations. While in business transactions or during formal interactions, presentations may also play an important role. We have to speak publicly more these days than ever.

Under such circumstances, it's the best to master the skill of presentations. Presentations look very reasonable and even persuasive but to serve its purpose, it should also be very motivating. People nod their heads and then mind their own business. So, when you are given a chance to deliver any presentation, whether in schools, colleges, or even at the workplace for any official purpose, try to make the best use of that opportunity to polish your communication skills and leave a mark on the people's minds.

Finding Context to Your Presentation:

Context refers to the information about why you are presenting. Every Presentation has a context and you must be clear on this before you do anything else. To identify the context of your presentation, try to focus on the situation, medium, subject, audience and the objective.

Few Questions to Decide before An Official Presentation:

Don't accept an invitation to give a presentation immediately. Your move not to accept the invitation immediately does not show your lack of interest, or shyness- It rather prepares you for the planning and evaluation before starting with the preparations. Before giving any sort of presentation, its best to mentally find out the answers of a few obvious questions:

1. Who Wants You to Speak, and What Organisation do They Represent?

At times, the person to contact you maybe an acquaintance, but it's vital to find out about the organisation, its contact details and values. This helps in setting up your own expectations and forming an idea about the kind of content that you would need.

2. What is the Planned Event?

It is vital to identify the kind of event where you are expected to be present. Knowing the occasion helps to identify the potential audience and the participation. The audience will be different as per the occasion, a sales conference, a technical meeting, a product launch event, etc, all will have a target audience. Here you need to know what has given rise to the presentation. Are you being assessed, perhaps either academically or professionally? Are you pitching an idea or proposal to a client? Were you assigned the presentation because no one else wanted to do it?

3. When and Where is the Planned Event?

This helps in preparing yourself, and getting an idea about the time that you have for getting yourself ready. How important is it and therefore, how much time and effort do you spend on preparations?

4. How Many Speakers will be Involved?

This helps you to judge the time that will be available for you to deliver, and also helps in indicating the profile of the event- its significance among the industry and the expected attendance. How important is this for your personal branding? How important is it for your success?

5. What is the theme of the Event, and the Kind of Presentation That is Expected from You?

This helps in getting the content accordingly. At certain situations, you might need case studies to assist in your presentations, while in other cases, you could count on the basic expertise and your experiences in the related fields.

6. What Visual Aids Can Be Made Available to You?

This is undoubtedly the most important concern, before preparing the content for any presentation. Find out about the method of delivery, for example: In a work meeting room with colleagues and a white board, or a video conference, a client's office, or at a conference with lectern and microphone.

This has implications for the equipment that you will use and therefore the types of visual aids you will produce, the level of interaction possible or expected with the audience, your dress code and how much rehearsal is necessary. Imagine a scenario, where you get the presentations in the form of slideshows, only to discover that there is no computer available at the last moment. Therefore, it is important to know the details beforehand. All these questions appear to be very basic at the ground level. But finding out the above answers is the very first step for deciding the quality of the presentation that you are about to deliver.

Set Your Presentation Objective:

Once you decide to take up the presentation, you need to follow certain basic steps in order to properly layout the content and set the objectives of the presentation. The most common mindset among people is to directly open the Microsoft PowerPoint Software and start designing the slides and focussing on the information, the visuals, etc. Such a focus is needed, but at an initial level, we just need to consider the expected outcome and the achievement. Consider the following points:

1. After the presentation, what will the audience DO that is different?
2. After the presentation, what will the audience KNOW that is different?
3. After the presentation, what will the audience BELIEVE that is different?

The three (3) points sound almost alike, yet identifying answers to them will greatly help you in creating a 'differentiation' factor that makes you unique. To be effective, presentations must have an impact that is greater than a simple e-mail, any business document or telephonic conversation. Direct face to face presentation has the effect to change the thoughts, actions and beliefs of the audience.

> *TIP:* Create a presentation mission statement, that helps to capture the planned expectations of the audience.

The mission statement should be a single sentence, to the point and succinct. It should be readily measurable and achievable within the context of a single presentation. A carefully derived mission statement helps in properly identifying your purpose and setting up the presentation objectives accordingly.

Examples of Some Mission Statements Maybe:

1. Ensure that the team understands the Human Resources impact due to the factory closure.
2. Ensure that the clients understand reduced pricing as a value addition to their product.
3. Convince the management about the need for a newer library in school.

4. Explain the students about the principles of Object Oriented Language.

5. Explain the teachers about the project developed during industrial training.

These are just some of the mission statements, which may form the basis for the presentations. Each of them is a measure, achievable, to the point and defines the intent for delivering the presentation.

Master Your Presentation Objectives:

With your mission completed, your next step is to build strong workable objectives. All your objectives have to be achievable by you, *the speaker* and they have to be achieved within the time permitted with the audience's attention. Once you consider the external pressures of time and audience, it is important that you have the means to deliver the best in the least possible time–workable objectives give you the means.

Having good workable objectives is an essential element of an effective presentation. Critically, they fulfill three main purposes:

1. Workable objectives provide you with a framework for success–giving you a quick overview of everything that you need to present.

2. Workable objectives stop you from going off message–at all times, when you plan, when you write or when you deliver your presentation.

3. Workable objectives get you to where you want to be –serving as visible milestones of progress made and distance still to be covered.

Well outlined and understood objective even helps the audience to understand the presentation's logic. They ensure that the audience is more likely to follow the presentation and remain attentive by the subject whatever that subject might be.

Example:

Ensure that the team understands the Human Resources' impact due to the factory closure. With this mission statement, you could expect some workable objectives along the lines of:

- ✓ Set up the chances for manufacturing optimisation.
- ✓ Keep check on the manufacturing progress by having benchmarks.
- ✓ Describe and lay the costings of the HR impact.
- ✓ Find out if any options are available as alternatives.

Your target should be four or five workable objectives that can be handled easily and smoothly. It is a common mistake to have multiple lists of objectives and issues at every stage. Too much detail at this early stage is not useful. It confuses the audience. Your workable objectives should be short, sharp and in tandem with the mission statement. Workable objectives might include: *research, develop, deliver, compete or gain share–action* words which are well understood by your audience and works best. There is no room for misunderstanding.

Activity:
Try to work out the objectives of the mission statements that are mentioned in the previous section.

Set Your Presentation Points:
How you choose to organise the presentation greatly determines its success in leaving a long lasting impact on the audience. It is advisable to set up a mission or a purpose for your presentation. The mission should serve one or more of the following:

- ✓ **Entertain:** To achieve more impact with your presentations, it should have a differentiation factor that distinguishes the work with others. Presentations must possess dynamism of its own, and a sense of activity that encourages the audience to be attentive and helps them to participate.

- ✓ **Inform:** Presentations are a chance to inform others about the progress, developments, enhancements, launching of newer products, etc. While designing such presentations, their content should be carefully monitored. The presenter should convey, explain and interpret not just the facts and statistics, but also their meanings and clarifications.

- ✓ **Advocate:** Advocate the cause- change, the new technology or the need for newer product, whatever the case maybe. Plead the case and try to change the opinion of the people by justifying your views with *logic, empathy* and *reason*. Example, advocating the need for a newer library in school.

- ✓ **Inspire:** When you have the opportunity to say something infront of an audience, it's necessary to make the best use of that opportunity. Your words have the power to animate others, and instill new energy and vigour on the people, by introducing *fresh thoughts, ideas and concepts*.

- ✓ **Persuade:** As a presenter, it maybe often needed that you use persuasive skills to convince others for a need to take some action. Say for example, in a Board Meeting for the launch of a new product, it maybe needed to convince the stakeholders to trust the potential of the product and invest.

The above mentioned purposes are not mutually exclusive. A single presentation may serve most of the purposes mentioned above.

Case Study:
Ms. Rita, was the Vice Principal of Alpha Beta School. Being concerned about the overall development of her students, she was well aware about the importance of current affairs and news. As a result, she made up a rule. Every day, after the school assembly, the students read out the news headlines in front of the students. They covered three headlines each from sports, business, international and national news. Daily, the students had extra 15 minutes of the assembly, an obligatory, 'News Headline Session.' Each day some unlucky student was appointed to inform the rest of the class about the latest developments in the world and it was a nightmare.

Analysis:

It was a nightmare not because the students didn't want to learn the updates. As a matter of fact, they did and quite passionately because they too could relate to the news. The problem was that the "political information" had no real purpose; it served no real goal. They had no idea what they were supposed to do with all this information. There was no space for questions and they didn't discuss anything. They 'just informed' each other.

So every day for several years, they had to get up and stand in the assembly for extra 15 minutes. For no reason and for nothing - I don't know why, but 15 minutes seemed a lot to the kids, especially early in the morning. They hated it. *Please don't inflict this on your audience. Please don't 'just inform' other people. Excite them, involve them, impact them and engage them, but don't just inform them with empty information.*

However, if there is no obvious need to deliver information in person, then staging a presentation may only be a second best solution. Therefore, always begin your preparations by asking yourself: 'Is a presentation the best way of achieving the required objective?' Check it against the following indicators:

WHAT DO I WANT THEM TO...

- ✓ Do people need to discuss the topic of the presentation in order to reach a decision?
- ✓ Do people need to be able to question the presenter in order to fully understand the material?
- ✓ Is the presentation designed to 'sell' an idea, a product or a course of action?

✓ Is there any kind of practical element in the presentation?

So never *assume* that a presentation is the only way or the best way to communicate information until you've considered all the other options.

Case Study:

Rahul was asked to prepare a presentation for some of the senior managers. Unfortunately, he was already under pressure to wrap up an existing assignment, and the time needed to prepare and deliver the presentation could seriously jeopardise the chances of meeting the deadline for the current project. He decided to review the situation and examine the real goal that he was being asked to achieve, which was simply to disseminate information.

Instead of preparing a speech, Rahul drew up a wholly adequate written description of the required information including half a dozen relevant charts and diagrams. The whole package was put together in a couple of evenings, typed up during the day – whilst Rahul was getting on with his other work – and was delivered to the head office, a couple of days ahead of the date of the now defunct presentation.

Analysis:

He didn't waste time turning hard facts into a speech, or rehearsing, or preparing visual aids, nor did he have to be out of the office for a whole day when time was at a premium. The senior managers also benefitted in that they were able to review the material at their leisure and didn't have to put off any last minute appointments that would have clashed with the presentation.

Therefore, clearly identify the purpose of the presentation, and look out if there are no other alternatives. Once you determine the purpose of presentation, there comes the phase to kick-start the planning process- to set up a theme for the presentation and bring relevance.

You can structure your presentation clearly. You can also prepare outlines and make the right points for your audience. When you get the right purpose for your presentation, everything else follows.

There may be many points you want to make. Write down all of them and then rationalise the list. Aim for three good points in your presentation. Having too many points will only lose the audiences attention, so aim to delete some points, edit them or aggregate them. Organise them in a manner that each point is self-standing, powerful and memorable. Each point should serve the purpose of your presentation and bring relevance.

Your three main points provide the basis for your presentation–its theme or thesis. Writing down the presentation thesis, the central argument, is useful for the next stage. There are three easy ways to organise your points.

   1. **Timeline**. A chronological order to your points might be appropriate. A rigid timeline works with a strong story, but it isn't always the best option

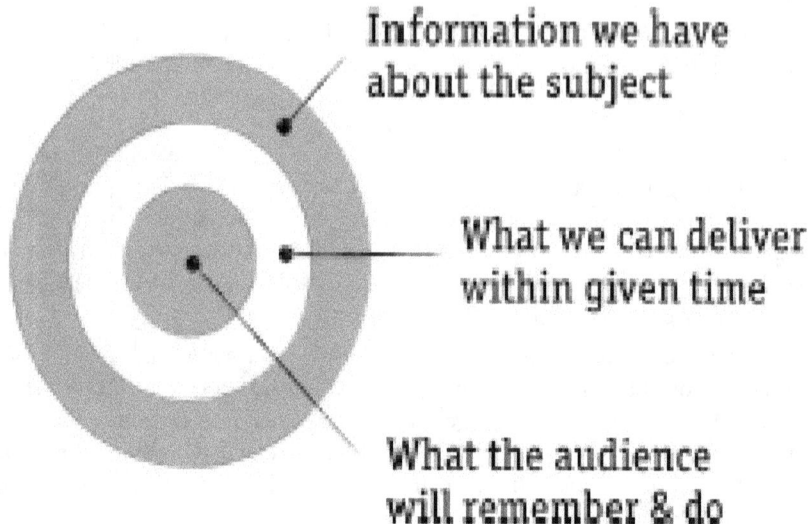

for a presentation. You could miss from the timeline at the last moment, or you might want to discuss further about any point. Have a vision of the future and then detail the steps needed to get from here to there. If you do mix up the chronological order, aim to explain each step very clearly. This way the presentation will be more organised.

2. **Tell them.** You might adopt the simplest of techniques in which you tell the audience what you intend to tell them. And then you tell them what you have just told them. It's neat and simple and it includes plenty of repetition of the main points. It's probably ideal for internal events, but it might be overly simple for external presentations.

3. **Problem, cause, solution.** In its simplest form, this organising method highlights a problem or issue. It addresses its cause, and it presents a solution. In reality, the problem typically has more than one facet. The cause has more than one dimension, and there are many solutions. But the problem, cause, solution and approach provides scope for more detailed consideration of your three main points and their supporting evidence.

Case Study:

Earlier, we mentioned about a case, where Jai had to give a mathematics session to the school students. In the beginning of the presentation, just after his introduction, he worked upon all these main points to deliver a successful session. "We know that maths is all about formulae and shortcuts. Unfortunately, there is a long list of formulae and it is difficult at times to memorise each one of them. We often get confused about their correct applications and thus, our fear for maths increases. I am here to help you all in overcoming that fear, and to give some handy tips and formulae for all the basic sections of your curriculum.

The best technique is to list out the most frequently used formulae and then practise to use them again and again. I will take a 2-hour session, which is divided into 4 modules of 30 minutes each. The modules cover important portions of *calculus, trigonometry* and *algebra*. In the 4th module, we will solve some questions to see the practical application of the formulae learnt during the previous sessions. We will also have a revision session for five (5) minutes on the completion of each module, so that you can clarify all your 'doubts and confusions.'

Analysis:

In the above case, Jai has already informed the students about the problem and its solution. He has clearly mentioned about the time durations and the module wise objectives. After each module, a *revision session* will help the students to brush up the concepts learnt. He has effectively conveyed all the desired information in simple and clear words. This way, the audience is aware of the agenda for the session.

Identifying Your Audience:

An effective presentation is a relevant presentation, and an effective presenter is the one which provides relevance to its audience. To be relevant in the minds of your audience, your presentation has to associate its title, subject matter, content and findings with the immediate care and interests of the audience. Simply, who is the audience – guests at a function, a lecturer, an executive team, colleagues or client? Once again, be specific and identify the names and titles, why they are there and how many will be in the attendance.

The value that the audience extracts from their participation in your presentation has to outweigh the costs that they incur in *their attendance–time, travel and reputation costs*. None of these costs can be overlooked–particularly, that of time which has the largest value. If the audience judges that their time is better spent doing something else or listening to someone else, then you have hardly been effective. When you know the costs incurred in participation, your task is to make the presentation as relevant and topical as possible. Aim to outweigh the costs of the audience's participation with your added value. Knowing your audience better is the first step in achieving relevance and getting to an effective presentation. Try to gather as much information about the kind of audience as is possible.

When you analyse the audience data, you can establish the outline for strong and relevant presentation content. You should now have a good idea of the particular interests of your audience, their requisite needs, their likes and dislikes, and their primary drivers. With this information, you can incorporate topical elements into

---

TIP: *You can even refer to former participants of an event, the event organisers or even other speakers to know about the kind of audience expected in the presentation. This turns handy to meet the audience's expectations during the session.*

the presentation's content. You can introduce the industry sector news and key issues into the subject matter. You can also make reference to the key figures in certain organisations or industries—you can demonstrate that you have a rapport with the people and concerns that fill your audience's working days. You can identify the tickling nerves of the audience and accordingly, use it to your advantage.

When your presentation is relevant, you are effective. You still have some way to go. You must still ensure that your presentation is useful and meets your mission requirements, but you have achieved relevance by knowing your audience. You are well down the path to mastering your presentation.

Try to Find Out the Answers for the Following Questions:

1. Who will be attending the presentation, and what is their level of seniority/importance?
2. Who is the decision maker (where relevant)?
3. Is there any point in giving the presentation if certain peopleare unable to attend?
4. Will people be attending your presentation by choice?
5. Is their initial attitude likely to be pro, neutral or anti?
6. How intelligent are they? *Never* talk down to the people.
7. How well informed are they? Will they have any background knowledge at all and, if so, how much?
8. Will they understand any jargon you normally use?
9. What sort of mood will they be in?
10. What will they be expecting from you?
11. How can you present your material so as to encourage a positive response (and avoid a negative reaction)?

Every time you can accurately gauge one of these factors, and tailor your presentation accordingly, so that your communication becomes all the more effective.

THE GOAL CONNECTS!

Identify the Filters and Motivators:

We have identified who your audience is above when looking at the context of the presentation. Do people automatically understand every word you say? No! In real life, there is always a 'communication gap' – the difference between what I *meant* to say, what I *actually* said, what you *think* you heard and what you *think* I meant.

This gap is particularly important when you are delivering a presentation. After all, the word, 'audience' is a *collective* noun. It appears to be singular, but it is actually shorthand for 'an audience of individual listeners'. And not just individuals, but individuals who have a wide variety of views on just about any topic you care to mention. We need to use a language that brings all these individuals on the same level, and is equally understood by them. This is typically needed to effectively communicate with all the people. We have to give special consideration to two things: How your audience filters information, and what motivates your audience.

Filters

Let's look first at how the audience filters communication. It should be no surprise that it's going to be different for you, and you need to be very conscious of this fact.

Case Study:

Jacob is a marketing head of a famous event management organisation, and his job is to convince his clients about the best quality services provided by his firm. In a meeting with a client for pitching in the contract of a high budget marriage, he said, "All the guests will be picked up from the airport in a luxury car, and will be safely dropped till the hotel." The client's confused looks clearly stated that he had made some mistake.

Analysis:

What could have possibly gone wrong, the simple sentence, "All the guests will be picked up from the airport in a luxury car, and will be safely dropped till the hotel." was straightforward and understandable. Yet the audience decoded it improperly and had many doubts:

Which luxury car will be used to pick up the guests?
Will the car be AC or non AC?
Will it be a private hired taxi, or some other car?
Which hotel will be booked for the stay?
Will all the guests be made to stay in a single hotel?
What will the guests do after being dropped at the hotel?
Who will welcome or assist them?

Although we can usually communicate quite easily without cross-checking every word, phrase and sentence, this example shows how much we take language for granted. Thus, we need to be careful with our choice of words.

Whenever you have a thought, you pass it through a filter - your personal

filter of how you see things, and how you see the world. This will be a reflection of your own values, where you were raised, your perception of the audience, what you think they understand, the language you use - which will sometimes be generational, your level of education and the context of the communication.

We then 'encode' these thoughts and 'deliver' them using visual and vocal cues. We reflect all those elements listed above and reflect them consciously or unconsciously in your physical communication. Then this communication is decoded by the listener using their filter which will most likely be different to ours. It's a complex process. But don't be overawed by it. The key is to look at things from your audience's perspective, and take into account by being aware of any major differences.

Take a Look at the Following Diagram..
Examples:
Case 1:
You may say, 'I'm very excited about this project' delivered with a lack of emotions

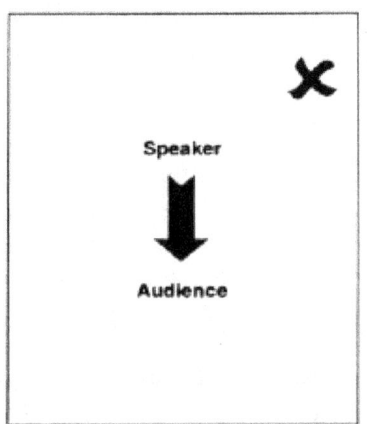
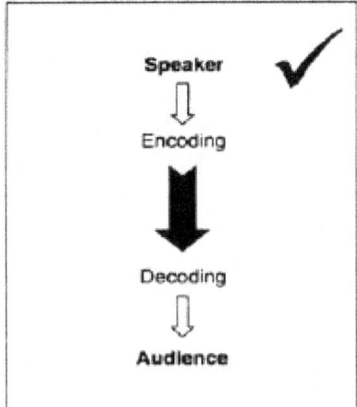

The communication gap

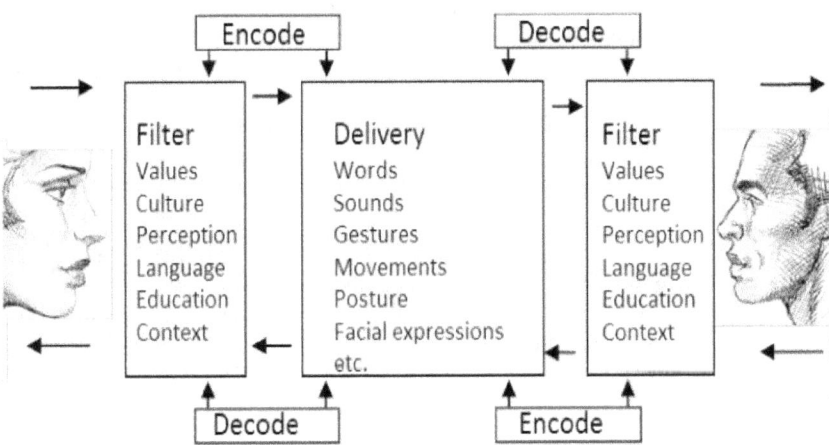

because culturally, for you, it's not appropriate to demonstrate emotions when you are communicating. But, they hear, "I just don't care about this project" because they don't share the same cultural values.

Analysis: By incorporating some simple gestures and small changes in voice dynamics, you can place the correct emphasis and create the right impression.

Case 2:

It can be the way you dress and the perception it creates. To say, "that's just the way I am, the way I dress" may not win over your audience if they have different expectations of how you should look. Suppose, while giving a presentation in front of your company's CEO, you dress up in a funky pair of jeans and T-shirt, it shows your lack of professionalism.

Analysis: Some small changes in this area and to think about things from your audience's view of the world will be rewarding.

Motivate Your Audience:

In addition to the understanding of communication filters, you need to understand what else drives or motivates your audience. First try and identify what the characteristics of your audience are and mark off the communication preferences that you will need to employ for each. First thing to note about this is that you only do this for the most important members of your audience.

Secondly, if you have a large audience, or even a small mixed audience then you need a more general approach which incorporates all these elements. The following table shows the various characteristics of the audience and the type of content that can act as motivation for them.

Characteristics of Audience	Example or Situation	Communication Preferences
Trusting, idealistic, helpful, modest, devoted, loyal, supportive and caring	To convince the people for fund raising in an NGO.	Use words of feelings and emotions, use facial expressions and body language, build rapport, use names, explain how they can help, be sensitive to their feelings, and articulate the value of relationships.
Self-confident, ambitious, persuasive, forceful, quick to act, competitive and risk taker.	During sales, pitch for any kind of business contract.	Use short sentences, give the headlines, get to the point quickly, emphasise action, accomplishment, results, action, demonstrate energy, enthusiasm and confidence, use words like absolutely instead of maybe, don't sugarcoat situations, give expected deadlines and be willing to debate issues.

Flexible, open to change, socialiser, experimenter, adaptable, tolerant, looks for opinion	While convincing for renewal of any official contract, you can use the information you already know, and highlight the work you have already done, to convince for further development of opportunities.	Provide lots of information so that they can determine the appropriate response, articulate the importance of their support for the group effort, show how others will be impacted, provide options and be willing to listen to options, offer a menu to select from and
cautious, reserved, methodical, analytical, principled, fair and persevering	While convincing the college authorities for construction of a newer laboratory, as the number of students have increased.	refrain from too much emotion and enthusiasm, provide the facts, provide detail, demonstrate your knowledge and competence, don't expect a rapid response. Be patient, give them time to think, ask questions, be rational, structured and sequential.

Creating Motivation

The best way to motivate your audience can be summed up in the question, 'What's in it for me?'

This may seem rather mercenary but self-interest is an incredibly effective source of motivation.

To make people take notice of what you have to say, you must give them a reason to listen, a reason which relates to their own experience. Talk to your audience as they are, not as you would like them to be. This, too, will benefit from as much audience analysis as you can manage. Some members of your audience may have been 'volunteered', rather than choosing to come of their own accord. Don't let this put you off. It may actually be easier to sell the presentation to those people if you can only show them that they aren't going to be wasting their time after all.

American psychologist Abraham Maslow has described what might be called a *hierarchy of motivation*.

The pyramid represents various levels of achievements. Maslow argued that people can only be motivated to move up to the next level when they have satisfactorily met the basic requirements of their current level. You are unlikely to have much success encouraging a company to embark on a major reorganisation when their most pressing need is to find enough money to pay their suppliers!

For maximum effect, then, you must *engage* your audience's attention at their *current* level, and then show them how your presentation will fulfill their natural inclination to move up to the next level of motivation.

Find The Evidence:

Collect all the evidences and information that will help you craft your message and help achieve your objectives. List only the information relevant to your topic. Here are some types of evidences that you should include with some examples.

Facts:

Months that begin on Sundays always have a Friday, the 13th. The sales department has about 3200 employees, out of which 1200 employees are from the MBA background.

Personal Experience:

After talking to our customers, I can say that our team needs a lot of work. I can say that the sale of winter wears is at its peak during the months of September/October.

Expert Testimony:

Professor Brown of MIT stated that the probability of a successful launch was 10%. "Apple's core strength of knowing how to make very sophisticated technology comprehensible to mere mortals is in ever greater demand," Jobs told a *New York Times* columnist writing a piece about the iPod in 2003.

Statistics and Samples

90% of customers were in support of change.
20% students in the college are admitted on the management quota.

Examples:

The following comments are a good example of our client's experience……
The same technique was useful in companies like …..

Analogy:

Running a business is like managing a theatre production. "Apple TV is like a DVD player for the twenty-first century"(Introduction of Apple TV, January 9, 2007)

Known Facts:

The factory never operates on public holidays.
A Leap Year has 366 days.

Reasoning and Logic:

It follows that if people can't listen and read at the same time, then we should not talk whilst they are reading.

The more you repeat any information, the more likely your customers are to remember it.

In addition to all the above, the evidence must be: *relevant, representative, accurate, detailed* and *adequate*, but is it enough to convince the audience and bring the desired effect?

The key is to become persuasive by including only the information that is relevant to your topic and the audience.

Chapter 4

With the "Find It" step of the presentation completed, it becomes easier to structure and organise your presentation as you only use the information that you know will help you achieve your objective. A well-organised presentation has a better chance of success, And a well organised presenter is also more likely to master his/her presentation. With well-structured points and a coherent central argument, your presentation will be understood by your audience. And, importantly, it will be remembered.

When preparing a presentation, many people begin with structure, pouring all that they know about their topic into the allotted time. But, what is actually needed at this stage is to review the content against your objective. Are you on track or do you need to add or cull information? Don't get to the PowerPoint as soon as you decide the goal of the presentation. Don't ever start building your presentation in PowerPoint or any slide-oriented software for that matter. You'll too quickly become caught up in the minutia of your slides. Such software ultimately force you to think linearly and you need to think hierarchically first!

TIP: First prepare a structure for your presentation. It will act as a baseline to organise any kind of presentations.

The Structure is the **roadmap**. It gives the audience the signposts and the presenter confidence in where they are taking them. Using a structure that is easy to follow will aid the audience in retaining the information presented.

At this stage, you need to prepare coherent outlines that assist to make the right points for your audience. When you get the right purpose for your presentation, everything else follows.

1. Gather opinions;
2. Publicise an idea or situation;
3. Sell an idea or course of action;

4. Highlight a problem (and seek a solution);
5. Pass on the information.

They should be treated as simple templates which can be adapted to fit the particular needs and situations. Feel free to pull them about and change them around. Always aim to create presentations in a way that will meet the needs of your audience and which you feel comfortable with.

In each instance, you should note the impact your presentation will have on the audience. Take some time to consider how your audience will feel about the subject after your presentation. Ponder what their views will be once you have finished. Think about how their knowledge might be enhanced by your presentation. And, if you are successful, think about what actions they will take following your presentation.

Now you should consider the points, you want to make. Inevitably, there will be several. Write down all of them. Initially, you might succeed with four or five. But any more points will not be remembered by your audience, so it's best to plan for brevity. *Basically, aim for three good points in your presentation:*

Once you have listed them all, you have the chance to rationalise the list.

Case Study:

Roy was asked to prepare a presentation for some of the senior managers. Unfortunately, he was already under pressure to wrap up an existing assignment, and the time needed to prepare and deliver the presentation could seriously jeopardise the chances of meeting the deadline for the current project. Roy decided to review the situation and examine the real goal that he was being asked to achieve, which was simply to disseminate information.

Instead of preparing a speech, Roy drew up a wholly adequate written description of the required information including half a dozen relevant *charts and diagrams*. The whole package was put together in a couple of evenings, typed up during the day – whilst Roy was getting on with his other work – and was delivered to the head office, a couple of days ahead of the date of the now defunct presentation. He didn't waste time turning hard facts into a speech, or rehearsing, or preparing visual aids. Nor did he have to be out of the office for a whole day when time was at a premium. The senior managers also benefitted in that as they were able to review the material at their leisure and didn't have to put off any last minute appointments that would have clashed with the presentation.

Analysis:

Roy understood the utility of focussing on the objective of the presentation. He identified the main purpose of the whole idea, and then decided what exactly he wanted to say. He knew his content well, and did not go for the traditional approach. He ensured to give this definition of primary objective some hard thought, and did not go on until he was satisfied that it is as precise and accurate as he could make it. Then he adhered to it.

> TIP: *It is not always necessary to give presentations. Sometimes you may look for other alternatives to convey your information. Give presentations only if it is unavoidable and necessary.*

If you do decide that a presentation is necessary, there are at least five or six alternative formats, depending on what you want to achieve. To decide which is the most appropriate, it helps to start by drawing up a description of your primary objective *in just one sentence*, as shown in the following example.

The main points of this presentation is to:

1. Inform all the members of the project as to the current state of play;
2. Convince the senior management that the flexi time system should be extended to include all the office staff;
3. Explain why the current production targets are unattainable, and to present a more realistic set of figures;
4. Motivate the sales force to get behind the company's new product lines.

Once you know what you aim to say, you are ready to determine what the presentation is meant to achieve. For example:

- ✓ To gather people's views – On a new product, on moves to reshape the company, or whatever; (Purpose 1: Gather infor mation)
- ✓ To make people aware of an idea or to describe a business opportunity – To gain support for some course of action, or to indicate that action will be required in the future; (Purpose 2: Publicise a newer idea)
- ✓ To sell something or to persuade people to take a course of action which they might not wish to take; (Purpose 3: Sell a newer idea)
- ✓ To highlight a problem – To seek a solution, or at least to minimise its effect; (Purpose 4: Highlight a problem and seek solutions)
- ✓ To pass on information – To report progress or promote awareness (without requiring any kind of response); (Purpose 4: To pass on information)

Now we need to set out the expected/required result of the presentation as clearly as possible. We will deal with each of the presentation points individually, and know more about their basic structure.

Purpose 1: Gather Opinions:

No matter *why* we want to gather people's opinions on any topic, there are certain basic targets that must be set:

- ✓ Everyone involved must clearly understand the nature of the presentation.
- ✓ Everyone must understand what input is expected from them.
- ✓ It is usually more productive in this kind of presentation to have a medium

to high degree of audience interaction – to have people build on each other's ideas.
- ✓ The presenter(s) must have some kind of yardstick so that they can tell when the presentation has achieved its goals (or at least, has gone as far as it can usefully go).
- ✓ The basic framework for such a presentation might look something like this:
- ✓ Introduce the presentation – motivate the audience.
- ✓ Describe what is to be discussed, why, and the required objective(s).
- ✓ Open the topic up for discussion.
- ✓ Summarise the outcome of the discussion.
- ✓ If appropriate, give some indication of the likely outcome of the presentation.

Example: Suppose you have to give a presentation to know the audience's views about the advertisement campaign for a proposed new shampoo. You might need to know the audience's suggestions regarding creativity and their opinion's about the requirements for new the ad. Introduce the purpose of gathering to the audience- to come up with innovative ideas for the campaign. Motivate them to think about the ads of other shampoos that attract their attention, inspire them to think more and put in their ideas for the same. Jot down all their suggestions, and get details like the expected length for the Ad, the concept or the theme for the new ad and so on. This way by opening the discussion in front of the audience, you can gather more and more ideas. At the end of the presentation, you can also present the outline of the new ad that includes all the points discussed in the presentation.

Purpose 2: Publicise A Newer Idea:

When presenting a new idea, your main objectives can be:
- ✓ To have the members of the audience clearly understand the new idea.
- ✓ To gain acceptance for the new idea.
- ✓ To obtain a commitment to implement the new idea.
- ✓ In order to achieve these goals, the basic outline of your presentation might look something like this:
- ✓ Introduce the presentation giving some idea of its purpose – including the need for decision and commitment.
- ✓ Describe the *need* for the new idea – does it represent sequential progress or diversification?
- ✓ Describe the idea.
- ✓ Describe the results and benefits which might reasonably follow the adoption of the new idea.

✓ Summarise the main points of your presentation and give clear guidelines on what people should do to support the new idea.

Example:

Suppose an ABC Corporation decides to computerise its **Attendance Management System,** and replace all the manual entries in the registers by a *fingerprint recognition technique.*

The presentation is conducted to introduce the employees with the changes. Tell the employees about the *new attendance management system* that is being implemented-highlight the benefits of the new system, like no more need for keeping log books on the reception, ease of record maintenance, etc. Since most of the employees may not be aware of the *finger print recognition technique*, so tell them about the new process, that the sensors will be installed at the entrance gates of the office building, the employees just have to touch their left hand on the sensor and their attendance will automatically be logged in.

After telling them about the new system, you can also tell them the details of the individual to be contacted in case of any concerns or issues that the employees may face after implementation of the changes. This way the employees are familiarised with the changes and will be willing to accept it.

Purpose 3: Sell A Newer Idea:

In a sense, *all presentations are a form of selling – selling information, ideas, solutions* and so on. In a *deliberately persuasive presentation,* you will need to include some or all of the following elements:

✓ The members of the audience must understand what is being asked of them.

✓ They must accept the need for the proposed action/actions.

Regardless of whether the audience accepts every word of the arguments, you are putting forward, they must be persuaded to *act* in the required manner.

This is potentially the most difficult kind of presentation and must be handled with tact. Nevertheless, a carefully (and correctly) structured presentation can anticipate any negative reactions and actively encourage your audience to 'buy in' to the proposed action rather than fighting against it:

Introduction: Briefly identify the subject of the presentation, with strong emphasis on any common interests that may be involved – to keep the business running, to reduce costs, and so on.

✓ Explain why *any* action needs to be taken. Be as frank and as open as possible. And if certain information needs to be withheld to protect the company's commercial interests, then say so.

✓ Explain exactly what action needs to be taken, and by whom, showing (if possible) how you have reduced any negative element(s) to a minimum.

✓ Emphasise the *positive* elements of the course of action.

✓ Summarise the contents of your presentation and call for an agreement on the proposals.

Example:

Suppose in a factory, the production needs to be increased on a short-term notice, as a new assignment is to be completed within the time deadline. This might require that all the workers put some extra working hours. This change is likely to bring a negative reaction from the workers, but it clearly is mandatory from business perspective.

So while giving such presentations, it is better to inform the workers about the benefit of extra work hours, you can also tell them about the profit insights of the proposed changes and can warn them about strict actions taken against the employees who do not comply with the newer factory timings.

The changes are necessary, but also bear the risk of employee dissatisfaction. So, such presentations must preferably be given by the senior executives, who hold respect amongst the workers, and the words should be carefully chosen to avoid resistance.

Purpose 4: Highlight A Problem and Seek Solutions:

When the key element of a presentation relates to a problem, we might approach it in one of three ways, depending on what we have to say about the problem, and what action (if any) we want from other people:

✓ highlight the problem as a matter of information;

✓ open the topic up for discussion and possible solutions; or

✓ offer a solution to the problem, for further discussion.

✓ In each case our primary aim must be to foster understanding of the problem, and in the last two examples we would also want to:

✓ discuss the pros and cons of the possible solutions;

✓ gain agreement on what should be done about the problem/solution(s). The presentation might contain the following elements:

✓ Introduction. Make it clear whether the presentation is intended simply to highlight the problem, or do you expect some kind of response from the audience?

✓ Define the problem (including all relevant background and 'historical' information).

✓ Describe *significant* effects of the problem – who and/or what it affects, how the problem makes itself felt, etc.

✓ What possible/probable consequences may arise from

– Leaving the problem alone?

– Attacking it?

As appropriate, the proposed framework may include:
- ✓ Call for suggestions.
- ✓ Describe solution(s).
- ✓ Recommend the preferred solution (and say why it is preferred).
- ✓ Call for decision as to which solution is to be implemented/what further action/actions is/are to be taken.
- ✓ Summarise the main points of the presentation and the discussion, and (where a decision has been reached) indicate what further action/actions will be taken.

Example:

TGB is one of the leading restaurants in the city. It recently opened its second outlet, and was expected to gain more popularity and clientage. However, the restaurant manager noticed that the number of visitors was not as high as it was expected. He organised a general meeting with the stake holders to discuss the probable causes of the problem and to deal with them.

He informed about the average visitors in the first outlet and then told about the the various reasons cited by the members in the meeting were the degraded quality of food, due to less number of cooks in the kitchen, the poor hospitality offered by the waiter, as the new waiters might be inexperienced, the lack of proper publicity about the newer outlet, as there was no advertisement in the newspapers of social media, etc.

All these problems were discussed in detail and solutions like hiring more skilled waiters, increasing the number of staff, paying for advertisements, etc were proposed. This way a simple presentation, which was designed well on time and involved interactive sessions helped in raising the profits of TGB by a fortune.

Purpose 5: Pass on the Information

The final type of presentation is the one designed simply to pass on the information – to report progress in a certain area of the company's activities, or simply to promote general awareness.

Just as all the presentations require a degree of salesmanship, they also aim to communicate some kind of information. In this particular type of presentation, the only purpose is to convey the information, and there is no secondary purpose. The presentation will normally contain the following elements:

- ✓ Introduction. Explain what the presentation is about, and what the members of the audience are expected to get out of it.
- ✓ Background information that gives context to the new material, so that it makes sense to the audience. This will make the presentation more enjoyable and the new information more memorable.

- ✓ A clear and simple description of the new information to provide the framework that will make it as easy as possible for the audience to accept and absorb the data.
- ✓ A second review of the information, but this time with supporting evidence/details, such as:

– facts;

– examples (as close as possible to the audience's area of experience);

– comparisons;

– statistics (but keep them simple);

– expert opinions (wherever appropriate).

- ✓ Summarise the information, showing how it affects the members of the audience. If the company is moving into new markets, will this mean more work? More money? Greater job security? Show the whole picture.

Example:

Suppose in the college internship, you have done a research on a new technology, say *nanotechnology*. You may be expected to deliver a presentation among your *peers*, or in front of the *teachers for your assessment and score evaluation*. In such presentations, it is relevant to first explore the technology from a broader domain- explain the meaning of the word, 'nano'. Then slowly move into the detailed description of the technology, laying emphasis on the practical implementations that maybe cited as examples. This way at the end of the presentation, *the audience will have a clear idea about the technology- its application and the whole concept behind it.*

Waving or Drowning?

By the way, when you use this 'mini-presentation' approach, it is important to let your audience know what's going on, rather than expecting them to understand it all by themselves. After all, if you are dividing your presentation into distinct sections but don't have appropriate 'signposts' along the way, then someone in your audience who loses concentration for just a minute or so at the wrong moment may refocus on what you are saying, find it has no direct reference to what you were saying a minute or two ago, and remain thoroughly confused at precisely the moment when you need them to be understanding exactly what you are telling them.

The solution is to treat each mini-presentation as though it was a presentation in its own right, with a brief introduction, a coherent internal structure and a closing summary. Thus, the introduction for the presentation as a whole should preview the entire presentation ('tell them what you're going to tell them'), whilst subsequent introductions should link the new section to the previous section only.

Likewise, the final summary should draw together everything in the entire presentation, but intermediate summaries should only deal with the material in the section, you've just completed.

In practice, the summary and introduction between the various sections work best when the summary runs into the introduction, something like this: *So, those are the five reasons why I think we need to take action/actions [briefly list the five reasons]. Is everyone clear about that? [The question is optional, of course, offering you the chance to clear up any misunderstandings before you carry on.] Now, with those reasons in mind, I'd like to look at the three courses of action that are open to us...*

The message is clear: To be truly effective, an event must allow the audience to see, hear and interact with the presenter and the presentation material. In practical terms, a presentation must:

- ✓ Tell them what they *need* to know;
- ✓ Show them as much as is necessary to clarify, support and enhance your verbal message;
- ✓ Create opportunities for interaction – and that means more than just allowing time for questions.
- ✓ According to various studies, we can effectively recall:
- ✓ 20% of what we hear;
- ✓ 30% of what we see;
- ✓ 50% of what we hear *and* see;
- ✓ 70% of what we do.

Some people find that they can work on all three elements of a presentation at the same time, while others find it easier to write the text, then design the visual component, and then plan the points of interaction. Experiment and find out which method works best for you. It really doesn't matter which approach you take, just as long as you end up with a fully rounded product.

The Sweet KISS of Success

For every thousand presentations that go on too long, only one or two will be too short. Very few presentations are literally *too short* (in terms of minutes and seconds), which gives a clue to the next secret of producing good presentations:

Kiss

In its polite form, this stands for **K**eep **I**t **S**hort and **S**imple.

- ✓ In 20 minutes (including the introduction and the conclusion), you have time for only *two* major points.
- ✓ In 30 minutes, you might make *three* major points.
- ✓ In 40–45 minutes, you *might* be able to cover *four* major points, but three points and a longer time for questions would be a better alternative.

Mike Weatherley, one of the producers of the BBC TV programme Business Matters, is on record as saying: "When I'm making a programme, I usually work on the basis that I can get three main points over in the programme." The fact that a professional TV crew with all the hi-tech equipment and years of expertise at their disposal can't get more than three points across in half an hour is surely a lesson for anyone planning a presentation, no matter how sophisticated their set-up.

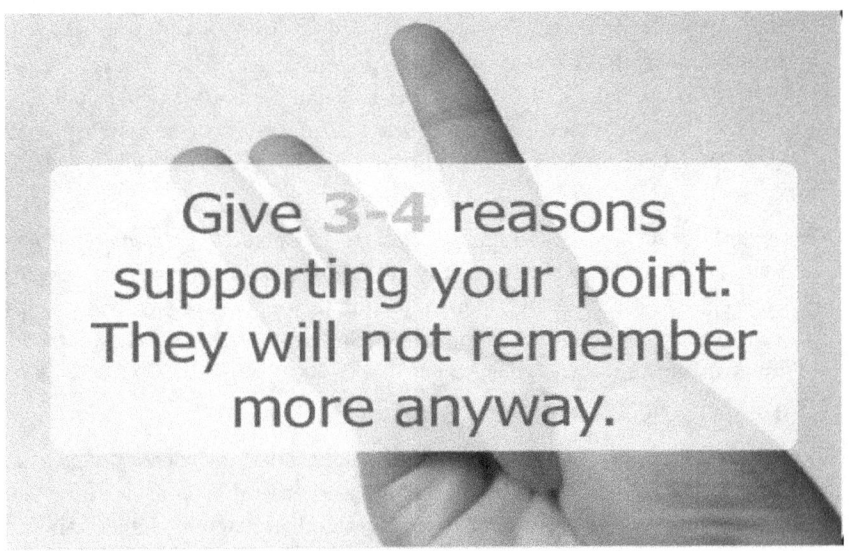

Most adults have an attention span of somewhere between 25 to 40 minutes, and can only process five to nine chunks of information at any given time. A presentation which contains too many items of information can be too long, even though it lasts for only 15–20 minutes. If you speak for much more than 45 minutes, it really doesn't matter how many points you make as most members of the audience will forget almost everything you say within the first couple of hours after you finish speaking!

You need to have the right amount of content, in a reasonable time span, delivered at an acceptable pace.

Use Titles for Your Presentations

A title can say a lot about your speech, and it can say a lot about you and your ability to speak on the selected subject. The title of your speech will be seized upon by your future audience. It might well be the only piece of information that they have about you before your presentation. Their decision to listen might be made solely upon your title. It's worth putting some time into its selection. *There are three good reasons why your presentation title needs your attention.*

1. It's a promotional tool that helps you to build the audience's interest before you actually speak. Your title will convey enough information about your subject to satisfy the appetite of your audience to hear more. *Stressing benefit and enlightenment–it's a sound promotional device.*

2. Your presentation title will also be used to introduce you to your audience. A conference organiser will reference your title when introducing you and noting your aptitude to speak on the subject. It's a very useful means of introduction. Plus it's a good device to demonstrate your subject aptitude.

3. It's the easiest possible way to build up a good introduction to your presentation. When you want a powerful beginning to your speech, your title will provide much of the clarity and vision you need. *The first 90 seconds of your presentation are vital* when you need to make an impact with your audience. When you need to set the tone for the rest of your speech, your title will give you all the hooks and links that you need to maximise this important stage.

4. *An apt title is one of the most important tasks you have when planning your presentation.* When you get it right, your title acts as a promotional tool for your speech. It acts as a good introduction to you, the speaker, and it helps you to make a sound beginning to your presentation. It's well worth the investment in time and effort to get that right.

Give a Theme to Your Presentation

When you think about a presentation, you typically consider the *presentation itself, its preparation, planning and rehearsal.* But it's also critical to consider how you engage your audience—how you actively encourage their listening, understanding and belief. Just standing on the podium and speaking won't do the trick.

Fortunately, there are some techniques that you can use and a major technique is the presentation theme. There are five things to bear in one's mind, though, when you use a theme in your presentation.

1. *Make it memorable.* Themes help your audience to remember your presentation. When your audience only retain some 10% of your speech, that's important to make it memorable. Themes are remembered by an audience because they can be. They work in much the same way as *logos, slogans* or catchy phrases. They are typically creative, clever and appropriate for the task.

2. *Keep it simple.* Your theme should be both simple and consistent. The simplicity is critical for memory—you don't want your audience struggling with complexity at this stage of the event. Consistency is all important. You should neither deviate from the theme during the presentation, nor be tempted to make adjustments as you go along.

3. *Be practical.* Your theme should evoke practicality and purpose. If it has these qualities, it will be familiar to your audience and prove more meaningful. Practicality suggests utility and benefit, and both are of interest to your audience. When your audience can sense the practical benefits of listening and engaging, their engagement increases.

4. *Be thorough.* There is no need to struggle for ideas when thinking of a theme for your presentation. There are many workable approaches for getting it right. You can talk to the *conference organisers.*

You can establish whether the conference itself has a theme, or you could identify if your particular day has a theme to it. In either case, you should aim to use this theme—or amend it to your own purpose. As an alternative, you can look at all the other presentations on the agenda, establish their theme and use it.

You could also think about some of the pressing work or professional issues that your audience will recognise. Examples might include: competition, globalisation, outsourcing, innovation or quality. They might be relevant and familiar.

5. Consider your objective. As you finalise your theme, you should recall the purpose or mission of your presentation. You are looking to achieve something with your audience:

✓ Change their ideas.

✓ Change their opinions.

✓ Change something that they do. Your theme should help you in this mission. *Both your purpose and your theme should be aligned.*

Your audience will only recall some 10% of your presentation. Your task as speakers is to increase that percentage or, at least, ensure the right, 10% is retained. A practical and memorable theme will boost an audience's memory retention and assist their engagement.

It's All in the Timing

People come to a presentation to gain information which will be useful to them in some way. They come to *learn*, and they need time to *absorb* the new information. Without that time, the information won't get past what is called the *short-term memory*, and will soon be lost.

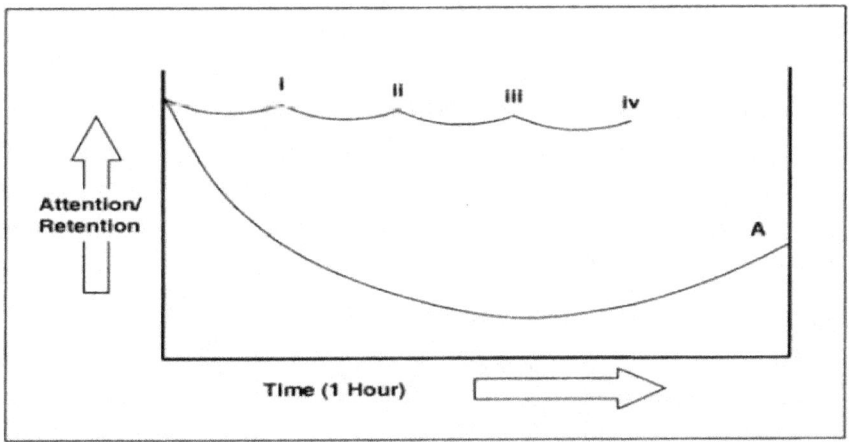

The lower line in this diagram shows how the increasing loss of concentration during the middle part of a presentation is directly related to the length of the presentation. Only the opening (*primary*) and closing (most *recent*) sections are retained to any great extent, and the recovery of attention towards the end of a presentation becomes smaller and smaller, the longer the event goes on.

The upper, wavy line shows the effectiveness of the same material – properly structured – when the presentation is kept to a *maximum* running time of no more than 40 minutes. It really consists of several 'mini-presentations', each with its own lead in and climax. The 'peaks' (i, ii, iii and iv) are built-in *high spots* at 10, 20, 30 and 40 minutes, which actively refocus the audience's attention, making it easier to maintain concentration *between* the peak points.

The One-man Think-tank

All you need for this technique is a sheet of plain paper (A4 is OK; A3 size is better), plus a set of coloured pens or pencils.

Lay the paper down with one of the long sides towards you and draw a rectangular box in the centre of the page with a line at each corner. (It is even more effective if you draw the central box and the four lines radiating from it in different colours.)

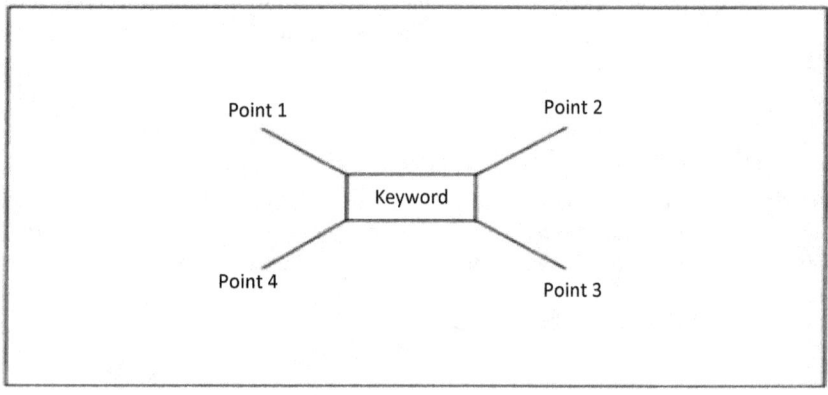

People who plan their presentations by drawing up a list of the things they plan to say often end up with nothing but a censored series of ideas – in no particular order. If we try to impose some order upon the list, drawing linking lines, for example; the end result is even more confused: The list arrangement (above left) is obviously very poor when it comes to showing relationships between points. The spidergram (above right), on the other hand, clearly illustrates individual points and the overall structure. What can only be inferred from the linked list is made patently obvious in the spidergram.

Incidentally, as far as setting out your spidergram is concerned, the following guidelines are recommended:

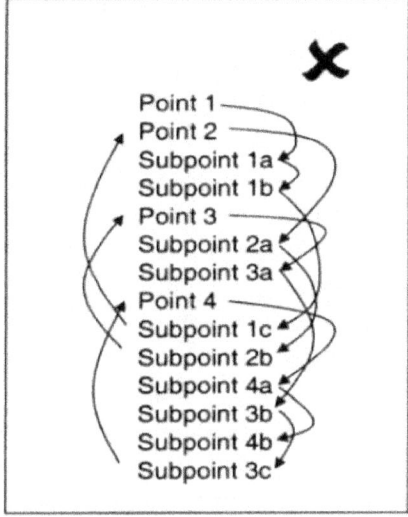 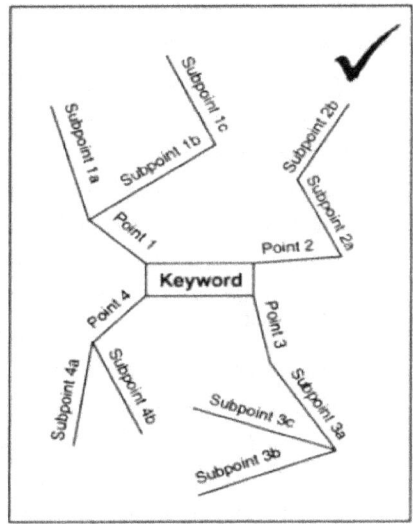

- ✓ The 'keyword' in the central box should be a one or two-word abbreviation of your primary objective.
- ✓ Use just one or two words on each 'limb', even a whole phrase if necessary – but *never* a complete sentence.
- ✓ Use the full range of colours, you have available with you.
- ✓ If different parts of the spidergram seem to link up, indicate this fact with a linking arrow rather than duplicating a whole set of 'limbs'.

Once you have completed your spidergram, you may need to do some serious pruning to bring it back to three main points. It will help to go back to your statement of objectives and start cutting out those parts of your diagram which aren't directly relevant to your primary objective.

Creating a Structure

Having assembled your ideas, the next step is to give them some structure so that the members of your audience get a clear understanding of the points you are making *as you go along*.

All too often novice presenters take the order in which they had their ideas and use that as the structure for the actual presentation. Sometimes, if they're very lucky, it works. Most times it doesn't, and the presentation is peppered with phrases like 'which I will explain later on' and 'I'd like to add some comments to something I said earlier about...'

One very effective way to create a structure for your presentation is to take the main points you plotted on your spidergram and write each of them on a *separate file card* or *Post-it note*. Then shuffle the individual sections around until you have what seems like a coherent sequence.

Next try reading through the sections aloud, preferably into a tape recorder, bearing in mind factors, such as:

- ✓ Have I introduced the subject clearly and in such a way that everyone will understand what the presentation is about and what they're expected to get from it?
- ✓ Does the presentation follow a clear sequence from the start to the finish? In particular, have I made sure that I introduce each sub-topic before I begin to talk about it – 'B will depend on A, which I described earlier...' is far better than 'Of course, B will depend on A, and I'll tell you more about A in just a minute...'
- ✓ Have you broken the information down into 'digestible' chunks of a size likely to suit the existing knowledge level of your audience?
- ✓ Do your closing remarks genuinely, wrap the presentation up and show how everything fits together.

Repeat this process, if necessary, until you are satisfied that your presentation meets all of these requirements.

All the Truth that's Fit to Present

People tend to respond more readily to upbeat presentations, so concentrate on the *positive* elements of what you want to say and the *negative* aspects of any contrary information.

There is nothing wrong in presenting your case in the best possible light, so long as you don't use distortions or lies. Having said that, you must also allow for people's natural cynicism. If you paint too rosy a picture and avoid *all* contrary evidences, your audience is likely to become more than a little suspicious. You can actually strengthen your case by including one or two possible objections – which you then demolish – rather than trying to pretend that no objections exist.

Think Ahead – Plan Ahead

Once you think that your basic script is complete, run through it with these *three considerations in mind:*

- ✓ Have you said everything you wanted/needed to say?
- ✓ Have you said too much?
- ✓ Have you left any obvious nooks for questions?

If necessary, you can now edit your script to resolve any obviously outstanding questions or ambiguous statements, and to remove any 'loose ends'. You can also script answers to questions that *might* be asked but which you don't want to cover in the presentation.

Script, Notes or Cue Cards?

"It usually takes me more than three weeks to prepare a good impromptu speech."

- Mark Twain

I once asked a particularly impressive speaker how long it had taken to develop such an effortless, flowing style. The gentleman concerned led me on stage and pointed to the *top of the lectern*, and some *20 cue cards*.

"No one can give a good presentation without doing the preparation", he told me. 'And very few people are skilled enough to work without some kind of notes.

'What you get from experience isn't the ability to skip the ground work – it's the facility to make it *look* like you didn't have to do the ground work!' So, which *physical* format is most suitable for your text?

Clearly, your presentation style should match your current level of expertise. How good is your memory under pressure, for example? It may look very professional if you appear to be speaking 'off the cuff', but how professional will it look if you say 'Next Monday' when you mean 'A week on Monday', or if you say '27 per cent' when you should have said '72 per cent'?

Some people really can produce a speech at the drop of a hat.

Most of us need some form of script.

Full Script

A full script takes time to prepare since it must be more or less word perfect. If you don't happen to have a professional scriptwriter on hand, you may have to produce several drafts before you get your script worded entirely to your satisfaction.

Using a full script can be a great *confidence builder*. You cannot forget your lines; there is no danger of leaving something unsaid or of giving incorrect information; and you can time your presentation with considerable accuracy.

On the minus side is that it is exceedingly difficult to *write* a script that sounds natural, let alone *read* a script so that it sounds natural. You must constantly break eye contact in order to look down at your script, and you are more or less tied to the lectern or whatever your notes are resting on.

A word-for-word text is also notoriously inflexible. If any part of your script needs to be changed at the last moment, you'll just have to cross out the obsolete material and make do with what is left – or learn to write very fast!

Notes

It is not unknown for a speaker to use a *spidergram* as the 'notes' for a presentation. It is more common, however, to prepare notes with main *headings*, *sub-headings*, and a brief *outline of each point* that you wish to make. In short, a rough guide to what you want to say.

Using notes means that you have something down in black and white (for confidence building), and in a format that can easily be edited right up to the last moment. If time runs short, you can use the same material, but simply deal with each point in less detail.

> *Tip:* Modularise your script.
>
> Write it so that you can add or remove material in neat chunks if the need arises.

Notes also allow you to *appear* more spontaneous, since you really will be speaking 'off the cuff', to a certain extent. The main drawback of using notes is that it is entirely up to you to remember what you meant to say about a particular heading or sub-heading. You will also need a place where you can rest your notes so that you can see them, but the audience can't.

Cue Cards

Since cue cards (for example, box file cards, approximately 10 centimetres by 15 centimetres) are much smaller than A4 sheets of paper, you will need to work with key *words* and *phrases* rather than sentences.

Using cue cards means that you can carry part of your script with you if you want to move away from the lectern. This will give you virtually unlimited freedom of movement.

The main drawback of using cue cards is the lack of written information. All the cards for a single presentation should fit easily into a jacket pocket or handbag. If they don't, your presentation may be too long, or you're putting too much on your cue cards. Perhaps, you would be more comfortable using notes.

Visual Aids as Memory Joggers

> *Tip:* To avoid getting your cue cards mixed up, number them distinctly in one corner, or punch a hole in one corner of each card so that they can be held together by a treasury tag or similar fastening.

Using the visual aids as an abbreviated script cuts down on preparation and allows a great deal of flexibility. But you will need to check each visual as you display it, which *could* mean that you spend more time looking at the displays than at the audience. You should also avoid making the visual aids more detailed to compensate for the lack of script or notes.

Foil Backing Sheets

If you have foils with backing sheets, these can be used:

✓ To carry a copy of the contents of the foil;

✓ For notes regarding the contents of the foil.

As your presentation skills develop, you may find that this is a practical alternative to the options suggested above. So the real answer as to how you should prepare your script is really up to you. Try each of the styles – *full script, notes, cue cards* or *memory joggers* – and see which works best for you.

Mastering PowerPoints

The first thing that comes to mind on being asked to give a presentation is a 'Slides'. A *slide* is a single page of a presentation created with slideware software, such as *PowerPoint* or *OpenOffice Impress*. A presentation is composed of several slides.

The *Microsoft PowerPoint* is a visual and graphical application, primarily used for creating presentations. With PowerPoint, you can create, view, and present slide shows that combine text, shapes, pictures, graphs, animation charts, videos and much more.

Creating Presentations:

1. Install Microsoft Office Suite, and we get the Powerpoint software.
2. Click the File tab, and then click New.
3. Do one of the following:
4. Click Blank Presentation, and then click Create.
5. Apply a template or theme, either from those built-in with PowerPoint, or downloaded from Office.com.

PowerPoint Templates are basically the *ready-made presentations* that require only the text changes. You are free to change or leave the images provided within each Powerpoint template as long as they are within that Powerpoint template. Most of the slidewares have Master Slides, which is another name for slide templates. They are used to give your presentation a uniform look. They establish fonts, colors, backgrounds, and positions for various elements of the canvas. If you choose your template wisely you increase the chance that your presentation will look decent.

Applying Templates to PowerPoints:

To find a template in PowerPoint, do the following:

✓ On the File tab, click New.

✓ Under Available Templates and Themes, do one of the following:

✓ To reuse a template that you've recently used, click Recent Templates, click the template that you want, and then click Create.

✓ To use a template that you already have installed, click My Templates, select the template that you want, and then click OK.

✓ To use one of the built-in templates installed with PowerPoint, click *Sample Templates*, click the *template* that you want, and then click *Create*.

✓ To find a template on Office.com, under Office.com Templates, click a template category, select the template that you want, and then click Download to download the template from Office.com to your computer

Inserting New Slides:

To insert a new slide into your presentation, do the following:

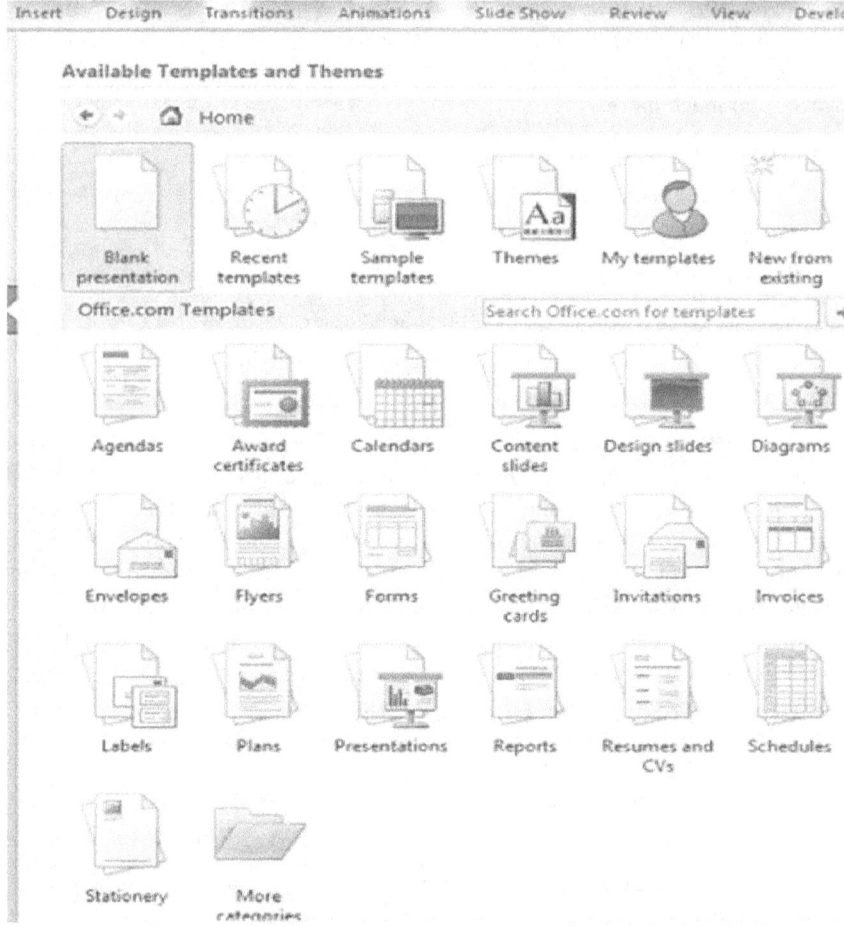

On the Home tab, in the Slides group, click the arrow below New Slide, and then click the slide layout that you want.

Even if you work for a large company in which slide templates are set in stone, it's still important to understand how templates are supposed to look. Sometimes, it is mandatory to follow the templates.

> *Tip:* You can also search for templates on Office.com from within the PowerPoint. In the SearchOffice.com for templates box, type one or more search terms, and then click the arrow button to search. - Box

Generally, people in large companies get tired of standard templates very quickly and start customising them to suit their needs and personal tastes. Unfortunately, most of the time, they end up creating something that's worse than before. There is no harm in bringing some minute changes in the templates, but ensure that the changes lay a

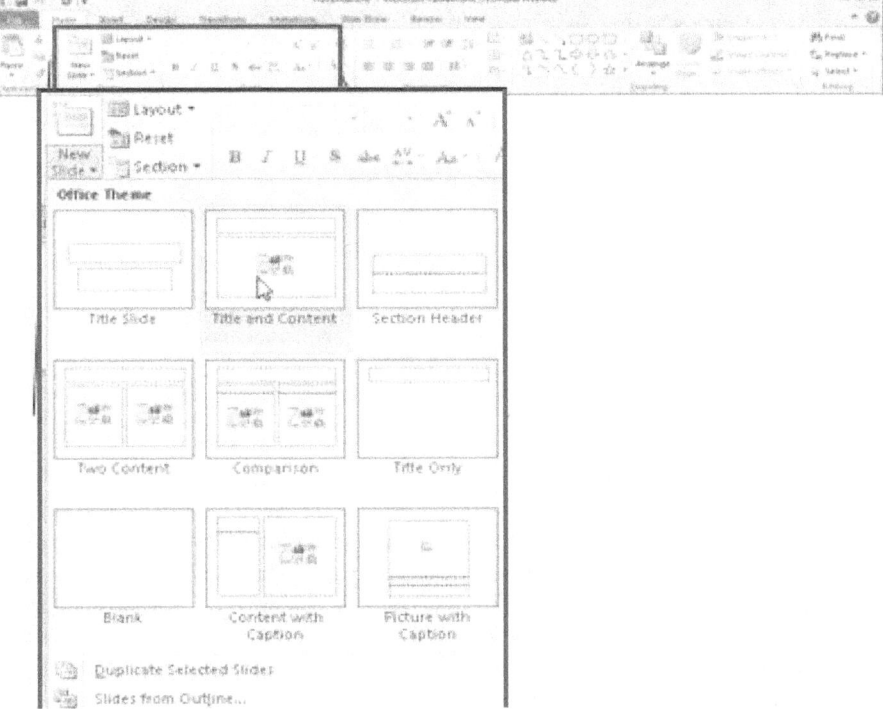

positive effect and are absolutely necessary to convey the information. If there's a real need to modify the template, then make sure the modifications are made suitably. A corporate style designer should have sufficient experience in delivering presentations and should be comfortable with PowerPoint guidelines.

Example:

The ITC Corporation organised a paper presentation contest. To maintain anonymity and a fair judgement, as a rule every participant had to follow the template of slides. The number of slides, colour scheme and also the duration of time spent on each slide was pre-decided and the same for all participants. Under such circumstances, to perform a winning edge, the participants had to bring some differentiation, while following the template. That needs *innovation and creativity*.

While most of the participants totally gave up on the contest, many of the people were confused about the methods to adapt for making their presentation different and noticeable. The people complained that the template provided to them was not very suitable for the event.

The Master Slide, which was designed for the contest is shown in the image below: The biggest (and most common) problem with this slide is the logo, in the corner which makes about 15 percent of the overall slide space unusable. This pattern can be called "a slide within a slide" because the slide space is divided between a number of different frames. For some reason, the designer thinks one slide is just not enough; they have to create an additional frame to achieve a look of sophistication and style. They just don't get how precious space is in this medium.

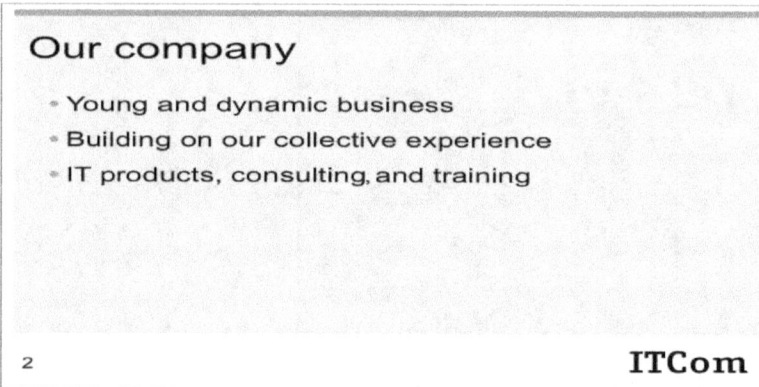

If the print is too small on a piece of paper you are reading, you can just bring the paper closer to your eyes. But slides are different. If you're sitting in a conference, your audience might not be able to just stand and walk closer. By closing off space, such "slide within slide" templates just require that everything else on the slide be smaller, thus alienating some percentage of the audience. It is always suggested to carefully choose the template, so that we can make the maximum utilisation of the space.

Some Sample Templates in Microsoft PowerPoint:

Look at the last template on the Figure above, the dark blue one on the bottom right. It's a copy of the Apple's template with a dark blue gradient background. This background is simple yet looks cool, especially in large rooms, where it blends with the darkness of the ceiling, producing an impression of a never-

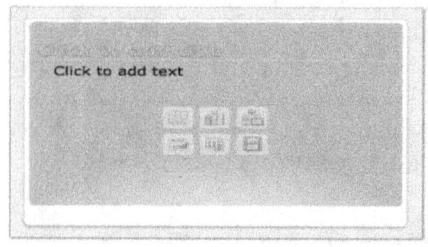
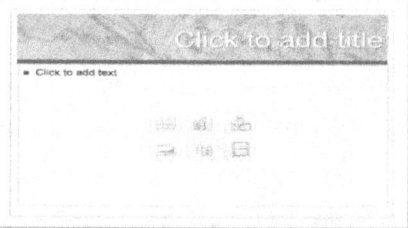

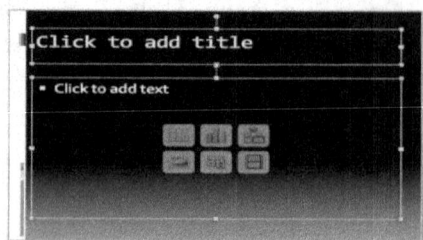

ending slide. Microsoft's version, however, has a bright white line on the left with some red patterns, supposedly mimicking film. This suppresses the effect created by the blue background and could be avoided.

Secondly, if you have a closer look, the fonts for the header and body are not the same. That's okay; you are supposed to have a contrast between header and text. But it is such a weak contrast! The difference in size is good, but the difference in colour is barely visible. Why have two colours when you can have one? What's the point? The fonts that were suggested were as follows:

This font selection was another mistake made by the ITC company.

The header font is called Consolas, and if one carefully notices, it looks very much like Corbel used in the rest of the presentation. However, this is a monospaced font, much like typewriter fonts, where all the letters have the same width. In most

Whatever   Consolas

Whatever   Courier New

Whatever   Corbel

fonts, different letters take different amounts of space. There are thin letters like 'i' and wide letters like 'w'. In Consolas, however, all letters have the same width. The fonts are almost identical, and thus, it brings no positive impact in the template. It's not very legible. Using a variety of fonts does not make any presentation interesting and catchy. If your presentation is boring, and you think some fancy background and frames can improve it—think again. This is not a design problem, this is a content problem.

Design is not decoration. Work on the structure of a presentation to make it interesting, design can just hold attention. E*verything* you have on your slides says something: every line, every border, every shadow, and every background. They communicate some information. Because human capacity for processing

> *Tip: Avoid using mono-spaced fonts, unless you have some serious technical or aesthetic reasons to use mono-spaced fonts.*

information is limited, you must ensure that everything on your slides communicate your message. A complicated design wastes not only your time, but also the audience's attention. *A good design communicates and solves problems.*

So what makes a good slide template?

Clarity: There are no unnecessary decorations, no huge borders, no logos except for the first and the last slides. All the branding you need is accomplished with fonts and colours. No noisy background. No rotating cogwheels in the background, no human faces, no faces of any kind, in fact. Here's a good description for your background: "It's white." No unnecessary shadows for headers, no word art, and no stroking and 3D effects for fonts.

Good Contrast: The body text is clearly visible on the background. The header text is clearly distinguishable from the body text.

Consistency: Different elements of the template "belong together," thus producing a consistent reality. For example, if the slides produce a scrapbook effect, there should be no 3D objects.

Example: The following template was designed by the *Apple keynote*, and can be taken as a good template.

The above template is simple, yet effective. There are no *superfluous design elements*. There's only one font and there are no borders! (Note that the border you see is just an element of the interface; it's invisible in the *slideshow mode*.)

Secondly, the header font is huge and bright, while the body font is smaller and paler. The audience can know what's important and what's less important right away here.

Thirdly, the background is just `grid paper' (and nothing else) and it matches the font. The asterisks, which are here used as a substitute for bullets also match the font and the paper.

Slide Layout

A slide layout is a template for creating slides with different types of content, so that slides of the same type have a consistent format. By default, any slides created after the title slide in a presentation will have *title and content layout*. This layout can be changed after the slide has been created, or you can create new slides which already have alternative layouts.

Changing Slide Layout

To change the layout of the current slide, click on the **layout button** in the slides group on the *home tab of the ribbon*. This will bring up the layout menu, from which you can choose an appropriate arrangement to display your information. When you have chosen your layout type, click on the *thumbnail of that type*, and it will be applied to the current slide. Any content that was already in the slide will be put into one of the placeholders in the new layout.

Layout Options

There are several types of layout available from the *layout menu*. A layout will change if you apply a theme to your document, but for all the themes, the elements included in each of the layouts are the same. *There are nine common layout options you can use in your slides. They are as follows:*

    Title Slide – This has placeholders for a title in large text and a smaller subtitle.

    Title and Content – This is the default option for a new slide. It has a

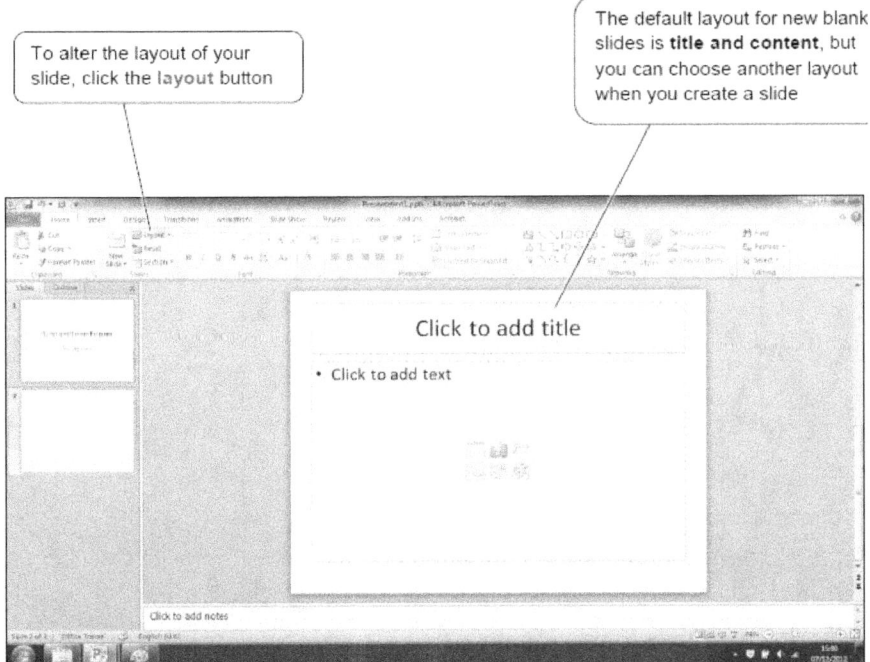

To alter the layout of your slide, click the layout button

The default layout for new blank slides is **title and content**, but you can choose another layout when you create a slide

title at the top and then a large placeholder for *content*. Any text typed into the placeholder will automatically appear as *bullets*, but you can change this if you like. Small buttons appear in the middle of this layout to allow you insert the *content* of other types, if you do not wish to use text.

Section Header – if you have split your presentation into sections, you may wish to use this layout to separate your sections. It can also be used as an alternative to the main title slide.

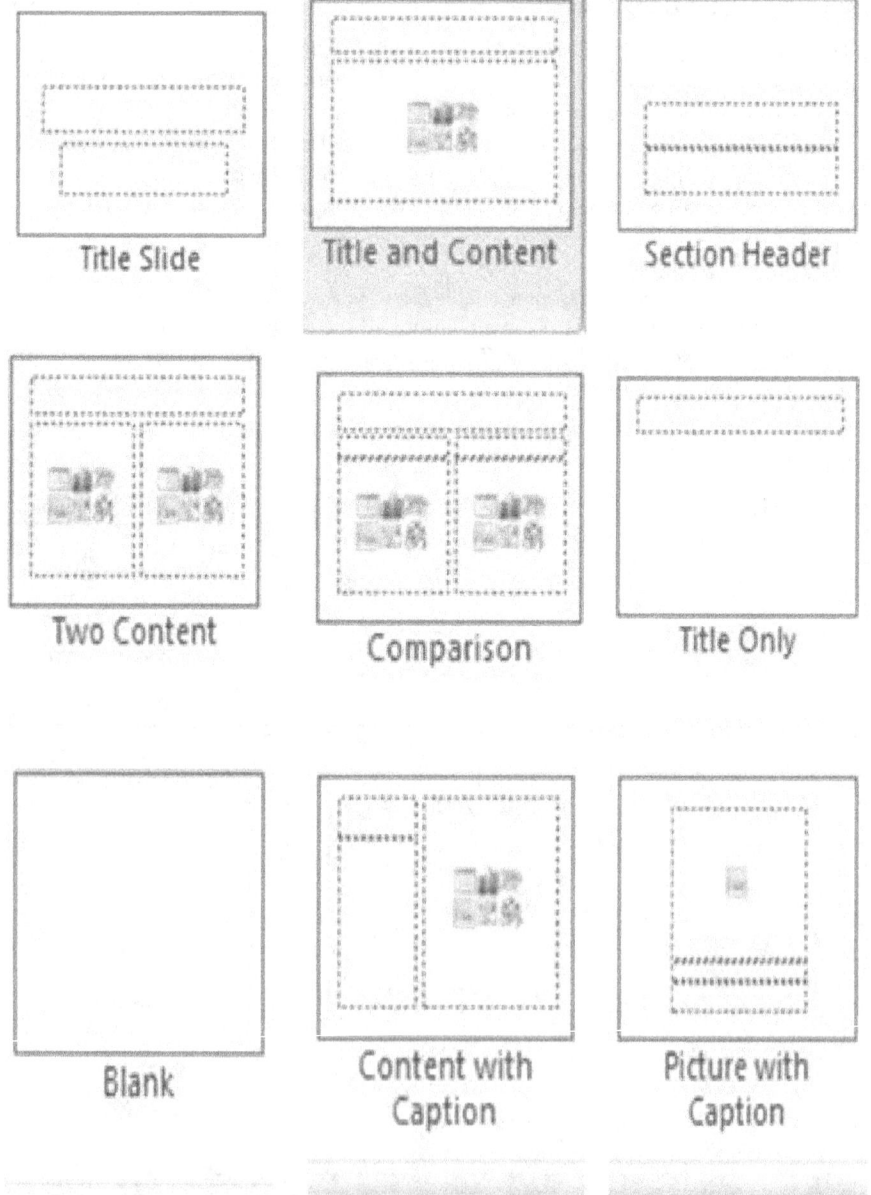

Improve Your Presentation Skills

Two Content – This layout has a single title and two boxes for content. You can place different types of content in each. For example you could put bullet points on one side and a picture on the other.

Comparison – This is similar to two content, as well as the title at the top, you will see two subtitle boxes, one for each of the two content boxes underneath.

Title only – This is a title page with a blank screen underneath. You can use it if adding a picture or diagram that you are copying and pasting from another program, or if you are using an interactive whiteboard, you can add a title and then have space underneath for people to draw or write in.

Blank – There are no placeholders for content on this screen, but it may contain footers if you have entered any into the master slide for this layout.

Content with Caption – This option has a small title and text box on the left, then a larger content box to the right to which you can add other items. Picture with caption – A large picture box is in the centre of the slide, and with an icon, you can click on to insert a picture. Beneath this, there is a small title box and a text box so that you can add a description for your picture. Whether the presentation is a simple text slide, or one with images, clip arts, etc. Whether the presentation is short or long, whatever may be the purpose of the presentation, in all cases, you need to ensure you have a clear beginning, middle and an end. Moreover, begin with the end in mind, so you don't move off the topic as you put all your information together.

This communication fundamental will hold you in good stead when organising your presentation.

Frameworks of Presentations:

There are *three frameworks* you can use depending on the length of your presentation. Depending upon the time of the presentation, we can either have a very short presentation (lasting 1-5 minutes), or a short presentation (for 5-15 minutes), or a long presentation (that lasts for an hour or above). Each presentation has its own value, and should be properly structurised, so that all the matter can be well conveyed within the stipulated time.

Case 1- Very Short Presentations

Purpose: Quick presentation or giving a clear instruction

Duration: 1 – 5 minutes

Visual Aids: Most likely none

Beginning: First tell them what you are going to talk about,

Middle: Then talk to them,

End: Then tell them what it was you told.

Example 1: Project status update

B. I would like to update you on the successful progress of the conference preparation.

M. We are currently on budget and on time. We have had to change venues however, but this has been quite smooth and all delegates have been notified.

E. The conference is shaping up to be a huge success.

Example 2: A conversation between two business people, responding to the question "what do you do?"

B. I have a very interesting job in market research at ACME Co.

M. I'm responsible for the generation of consumer insights into how we can better position our brands.

E. I find market research very stimulating.

Case 2-Short Presentations

Purpose: Most office presentations and some client presentations

Duration: 5 -15 minutes

Visual Aids: very few, depending on the topic, perhaps 3 – 4 maybe enough.

B: Give a brief hello saying to whom the message addressed (there are people involved – *so use the terms that motivate them to listen attentively*, also give an overview, an action step, a headline and an outcome.

M: Give the steps involved and any specific actions etc. , so that they know what all actions have taken place.

E: Sum up with next step or main points. Give indication about the people impact or people, the actions which are necessary.

Example:

For a presentation, given to the Finance team, informing them about the company expenses and the growth, the layout maybe as follows:

B. Thank you for your time today, it's always a pleasure presenting to the finance team. I wanted to give you a quick overview of where our expenditure is now and where we see it going in the next six months so you can project with confidence the company result for this financial year.

M. Our expenditure to date is $750k over budget; however you need to note that this was due to three factors, one an unbudgeted increase in the cost of promotional fulfilment due to a competition we ran that exceed expectations - $250k. Second some additional market research the CEO requested be undertaken into venturing into new Asian markets – 300kxx and finally some unbudgeted legal expenses associated with a product recall which was $200k

E. So at the end of the financial year, we will be able to curb the expenditure by $750 and be in line to meet the *sales budget* and *expenses*, which will be a fantastic effort by the sales and marketing department under tough conditions. We hope for sustained cooperation and hardwork in the next quarter from the team, so that we are able to accomplish the projected targets.

Case 3-Long Presentations:

Purpose: Influence or persuade

Duration: 20-60 minutes

Visual Aids: 1 per 5 minutes
Beginning: 1. Subject & 2. Agenda

Middle: 3. Body

End: 4 Summary & 5. Conclusion

The long presentation has five parts, as outlined above and are expanded upon in the Presentation Structure Sheet or Planner.

The planner is the sheet that you use when organising your presentation. It is comprised of *descriptions, numbers and arrows.*

The main components of a presentation planner are:
1. Descriptions
2. Arrows
3. Numbers

1. Descriptions

Audience: Key personnel, titles and important filters and motivation.

Presentation Planner

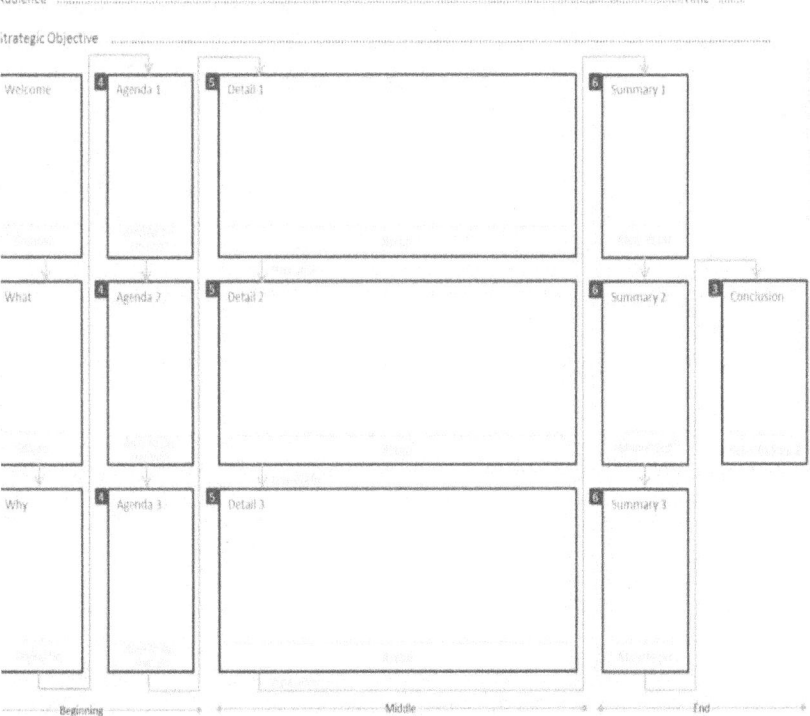

Time: How much presenting time, question time and buffer will you allow.
Strategic Objective: What do you want the audience to think and do differently after the presentation.

Welcome*:* The purpose of a presentation welcome is to put people's minds at rest. For short presentations, it may be your name and the duration of the presentation. For longer presentations, you may also include the appropriate time to ask questions, whether there will be any breaks, and where the amenities are.

Creative*:* The purpose of the creative is to produce a memorable context for the presentation. This may be in the form of a short story, a joke or some imagery. The key to a "creative" is making it concise and relevant to the presentation.

What*:* The 'what' is the topic or subject that you are there to present. It is short and to the point.

Why*:* The 'why' or objective also needs to be concise and to the point. Here you state how you anticipate the audience will benefit from your presentation.

Agenda: This is where you write down the topics or the areas that you are going to cover in your presentation. Once again these descriptions need to be concise. For presentations of any length, the agenda items would not exceed more than four to five key areas and no longer than 4 or 5 words long. The agenda gives the signposts for the presentation. It lets people know where you are going and therefore, enables them to focus on what you are saying. People often fall into the trap of saying 'before we start, I will just give you some background'. If the background is required, then this is your first agenda item.

Body: For each of the agenda items, there is a corresponding body. This is where you place all the descriptive and persuasive information. Here you can afford to be wordier, although we are still only jotting down the key points. We can also begin to think about what type of *charts, slides* or other *visuals* are required.

Summary: For each respective agenda and body item, there is a corresponding summary. The summary is the key message or main point that you want your audience to take away from your presentation. As with the agenda, the summary is concise.

Conclusion: The conclusion will typically reflect in a more decisive form, the objective stated earlier on. The conclusion may also reflect the main point or the next step required of the audience. If it hasn't been done already, you may field questions.

All that is left to do now is to thank the audience.

2. Numbers

These numbers represent the order in which you write your presentation, not deliver it that comes next. Begin with the end in mind. In other words, work backwards from where you want to end up. So in this planning sheet, you observe the following order of preparation:

1. Subject, to be expressed clearly
2. Objective concisely stated or alluded to
3. Conclusion, written with your objective in mind
4. Agendas, break your presentation down into sequential parts
5. Body, fill in the body of the presentation with relevant and persuasive information
6. Summary, from point 5, distilell the key message that you want your audience to take away from each body item
7. Welcome, write your opening remarks making them brief and construct an optional creative

3. Arrows

Now that you have written the presentation, the order in which you present is shown by the arrows. It makes sense that you would start with a welcome, then tell your audience what you are there to talk about - your subject, and then state your objective.

We then give your audience the *signposts* - which are your *three to five agenda items*. An error that is often made is to move across the planner giving each agenda item followed by the *body and the summary*. The correct way is to move down the planner listing the agenda sequentially; agenda 1, then agenda 2 and then agenda 3, etc.

At this stage, you have completed the beginning phase of your presentation and you are now moving into the middle phase. Each body item is now discussed with as much detail as necessary in order to reach your objective. It is also necessary to transition between or link each body to the next so that your audience can follow you.

After completing the body of the presentation you are now in the end phase. We commence this phase by giving your summary or the key messages which are derived from each of the respective body items. Once again you list these sequentially as you did with the agenda moving down the planner.

The last part of the end phase is to give your conclusion, instructions for any next steps and to field any questions.

Structuring a Key Message

You'll often hear, "what's your key message?" Quite simply a key message is a phrase that represents the main idea you want to express to the audience.

Your message will depend on all the things we have spoken about so far. Likewise, when you give your key message, it will depend on your type of audience. Some will want to hear it in the beginning only, to identify your conviction or belief in what you are saying, in which case, it would replace the objective.

Others prefer to know your key message at the end, after they have evaluated everything you have presented, in which case it would become the conclusion. As you saw in the planner, you may also have a number of key messages which form the summary of longer presentations.

To construct a key message, revisit your overall or strategic objective – what thoughts and actions are you looking to change in your audience. Think about your audience, their communication preferences, their position in the organisation, and their expectations from you. Now apply *the six sigma—5 whys technique.* For example, if you are recommending in your presentation that advertising and promotional (A & P) expenditure be maintained, then it may go something like this. The A&P should be maintained:

Why –So we can achieve our sales budget

Why –So we can maintain the market share

Why –Because we did it last year and the trade expect it

Why –Because we will be deleted by the retailers if we don't

Why–It's an important part of our brand portfolio

From here, you can develop your key message by incorporating each answer or perhaps, the most relevant among your objectives. So the key message at the beginning of your presentation that replaces your objective may sound something like this.

"We recommend that the A&P expenditure should not be cut and kept at the last year's levels in order to maintain the sales and market share and ensure, we maintain ranging, as product, xyz is a vital and profitable part of our brand portfolio. I will now demonstrate why we have drawn this conclusion." Structurise your presentation in such a manner, that it leads the audience to the key message and explains the relevant details in an easy flow.

Slide Sorter

Slide sorter view in PowerPoint or OpenOffice Impress is a window that displays thumbnail versions of all your slides, arranged in horizontal rows. This view is useful to make global changes to several slides at one time. Rearranging or deleting slides is easy to do in *Slide Sorter View.*

The slide sorter can be used for the following:

1. Completing a rough sketch of what slides you are going to use
2. Planning who is going to speak when and on what
3. Working out when different visual aids will be introduced and in what sequence.

Example:

In the given image, the Slide Sorter View makes it handy to organise the slides, their sequence and the time that is dedicated to each slide. Depending upon the significance and the content mentioned in the slides, the duration of time and focus spent on its presentation maybe varied.

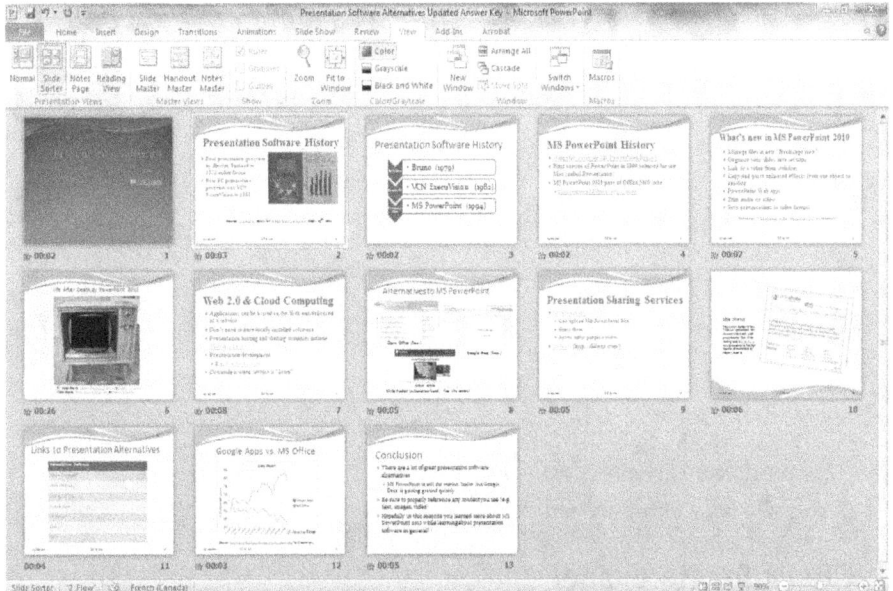

Summary:

Whether your presentation is short or long, you need to ensure that you have a clear *beginning, middle and an end*. This communication fundamental will hold you in good stead when organising your presentation.

Begin with the end in mind, so that you don't move off the topic, as you put all your information together. When you organise your presentation, you present more efficiently. Your delivery will be better. Your pacing and timing will be well-tuned. And, best of all, your audience will appreciate your investment with a better response to your spoken words. It's worth the effort.

Organise It

Chapter 5

this by doing three things; checking for relevance, choosing your words carefully and being articulate.

Check for Relevance

At this point, you need to review what you have done so far. We need to ask the following questions:

> Have you correctly diagnosed the audience, fully understanding their expectations, needs and motivators?
>
> Is all the information you have included relevant?
>
> Does the information flow?
>
> Are your recommendations persuasive – is their sufficient evidence?

Setting a Mood

How do you want your audience to feel as the presentation starts? Relaxed? Alert? Critical? Receptive? Your opening remarks will play a crucial role in setting the mood of the whole presentation. Would you open a presentation with a shocking statistic or statement, if you wanted the audience to feel relaxed and receptive? Would you try to stir your sales force to greater efforts by the use of soft lights and a 'fireside chat'?

For maximum effect, you must analyse your audience as far as possible, and then make a best guess as to what kind of approach will produce the required response from that particular set of people. Above all, *never* assume that any two audiences will react the same way to the same material; they won't.

Choose Your Words Carefully

Words are the building-blocks of your sentences, therefore you must have an adequate supply of words to construct your presentations. When your vocabulary is limited, you need to make a concerted effort to improve it. Your vocabulary will naturally increase as your experience and education deepens, but you can make vast improvements by reading as much as you can and by referencing dictionaries and thesauruses.

It follows that your diction must first of all be intelligible to your audience. It will be mainly the audience that will determine whether you can use formal or informal language. The audience, the subject matter, the occasion, and your purpose constitute the criteria for judging the appropriateness of your diction.

Vocabulary

If your presentations are confusing, convoluted, and full of jargon, you will miss an opportunity to engage and excite your listeners. Strive for understanding. Avoid lexical density. Don't be afraid of using simple words and descriptive adjectives.

If you genuinely find a product "amazing," go ahead and say so. After all, if you're not excited about it, how do you expect the audience to be? The words chosen should be simple, concrete and emotionally charged.

✓ **Simple:** Free of jargon and with few syllables.

✓ **Concrete:** Very specific phrases. Short, tangible descriptions instead of long, abstract discussions.

✓ **Emotional:** Descriptive adjectives

Example:

It was hard to miss financial guru, Suze Orman in 2008 and 2009 when the global financial markets were collapsing. In addition to appearing on her own, CNBC show, the bestselling author was a frequent guest on shows such as, 'Oprah' and 'Larry King Live.' Banks and financial companies were also using her in advertisements meant to alleviate their customers' fears. Orman was once asked - "How do you make complicated financial topics easy to understand?"

Orman responded, "Too many people want to impress others with the information they have, so others think the speaker is intelligent." "If your message is too simple, don't you risk not being taken seriously?" The interviewer was puzzled.

"I don't care what people think about it. All I care about is that the information I'm imparting empowers the listener or reader of my material .If your intention is to impart a message that will create change for the person listening, then if you ask me, it is respectful to that person to make the message as simple as possible. For example, if I gave you directions to how to get to my house, you would want me to give you the simplest directions to get there. If I made it more complicated, you would not be better off. You might get aggravated and give up. If it were simple, chances are you will get in your car and try to get to my house rather than giving up and saying it's not worth it."

Others criticise simplicity because they need to feel that it's more complicated. If everything were so simple, they think their jobs could be eliminated. *It's our fear of extinction, our fear of elimination, our fear of not being important that leads us to communicate things in a more complex way than we need to.*

Language is intended to stir up excitement and create a "must-have" experience for the audience. There's nothing wrong with that. Keep in mind that the majority of business language is dull, abstract, and meaningless. Inject some zip into your words to make it interesting!

Use the language of the organisation. If it's an internal presentation, this shouldn't be onerous unless you're new to the organisation. If it's an external presentation to a prospective client, make sure you use the language that is relevant to them. For example, do they refer to their end users as clients, patrons, customers or the trade?

Tip: Avoid using jargon.

Precision

Language can be so imprecise, knowing how to use it skilfully – Knowing when to be vague and when to be precise, and how to do this without making it painfully obvious to your audience – can be a valuable addition to any presenter's 'toolkit'.

Five of the key factors which identify 'vague' language are:

Undefined Nouns

What is missing in this undertaking: 'If necessary we will provide transport'? What's missing is a definition of the word 'transport'. Does it mean a hire car, a lorry, a bicycle or a pogo stick?

Undefined Verbs

The same principle applies if you get an instruction such as: 'We want you to come to the Mumbai.' *How* are you supposed to 'come to Mumbai'? By plane, by train, by car or on foot? And incidentally, who will be paying for this trip?

Undefined Comparisons

'Our new product is bigger and better.' But 'bigger' and 'better' than what? Even the apparently more precise 'Our new product is now the best on the market' leaves several important questions unanswered: 'best' as measured by what criteria? What market, precisely? And so on.

Unsubstantiated Rules

'We have to do it this way.' Why, just because you've always done it that way before? What will happen if you use a different approach? Does it have to be done 'this way' even if 'this way' doesn't work?

Unattributed Quotes

'All the research shows...', 'There was a study that came out last year...'. Who were these researchers? Who did the study, and working to what guidelines? Was the research really directly related to the area being discussed?

It is all too easy to attach our own meanings to other people's words and then assume that they actually meant what we think they meant. This makes it especially important that we do whatever we can to make sure that when we're answering questions, we really understand what is being asked of us.

You may also want to check your own scripts or notes to see whether the degree of precision in your language is appropriate to your purpose.

Be precise and don't generalise in your presentation. For example say "we had a 20% increase in sales not a massive lift in sales". Say "the strategy was successful for the following reasons", not "the strategy was a huge success". Say "the report will be completed by 2.00pm Wednesday", not "you'll have the report on time".

Pronunciation

Some people care a lot about the way we pronounce words. Rightly or wrongly you need to pay attention to your pronunciation. Author Julia Glover identifies ten of her pet hates as follows;

Ask not axe, Athlete not Ath-a-lete, Et Cetera not Ekcetera, Mischievous not MischievEEous, Picture not Pitcher, Specific not Pacific, Supposedly not Supposably, Anyway not Anyways, Cache not kashay.

Be Articulate

> **TIP:** *There are a number of excellent books of quotations on the market, but be sure to select a quote that is appropriate, and from someone who will have credibility with your audience:*

Another way to add zip to your language is to create analogies, comparing an idea or a product to a concept or product familiar to your audience.

'As Winston Churchill once said...'

'As Mabel Ramsbotham once observed...'

Most people have at least a vague idea that Winston Churchill was someone famous and important. But who cares what Mabel Ramsbotham once observed? Unless, of course, she is a well-respected colleague, a department head or the managing director, in which case her opinion may well count for a lot more than the thoughts of Winston Churchill.

Your listeners and viewers are attempting to categorise a product— they need to place the concept in a mental bucket. Create the mental bucket for them. If you don't, you are making their brains work too hard, the brain wants to consume the least amount of energy. That means it doesn't want to work too hard to figure out what people are trying to say. The brain takes shortcuts whenever it can." Analogies are shortcuts.

Nothing will destroy the power of your pitch more thoroughly than the use of buzzwords and complexity. You're not impressing anyone with your 'best-of-breed, leading-edge, agile solutions.' Instead, you are putting people to sleep, losing their business, and setting back your career.

Clear, concise, and 'zippy' language will help transform your prospects into customers and customers into evangelists. Delight your customers with the words you choose! The following are some examples of ways to make your presentation more delightful. It is not suggested that you use all of these but incorporating one or two will make your presentation a little more engaging.

Alliteration

Alliteration is the repetition of a particular sound in the prominent lifts (or stressed syllables) of a series of words or phrases.

Examples: Back to the basics, balance the books, boom or bust, making magic, pay the price, it takes two to tango.

Analogy

Analogy refers to a similarity between like features of two things, on which a comparison may be based.

Examples: Self-regulation for telecommunication companies is like putting students in charge of marking their own exams.

Apple TV is like a DVD player for the twenty-first century iPod Shuffle is smaller and lighter than a pack of gum. When you find an analogy that works, stick with it. The more you repeat it, the more likely your customers are to remember it.

Anecdote

An anecdote is a short and amusing or interesting account, which may depict a real incident or person.

Example: A friend visiting from interstate was baffled by our train ticketing system. Rather than being helped, she received a fine for not having the correct ticket.

> *TIP: Anecdotes must be very appropriate, and brief, to justify their use. In an event from quite some time ago, the speaker opened his presentation with a personal anecdote that started: 'You know, I nearly didn't live long enough to make this presentation... At that moment he had the unqualified attention of everyone in the room. By the time he struggled to the end of the story, some three or four minutes later, most people in the audience were thinking, 'So what?'*

Humour

There are two basic forms of humour – *instinctive* and *deliberate*. Instinctive humour grows out of the presentation material.

Deliberate humour, on the other hand, encompasses jokes, funny stories, cartoons and so on. But one needs to be very selective about the jokes used during presentation.

One genuinely funny, *relevant* story will work far better than half a dozen jokes. The important questions to ask yourself about *any* kind of humour are:

Will people understand it (as you intended it)?

Will they find it funny?

If you're not sure on either count, try something else.

Appeal

To a sense of justice: Small businesses need to be able to have the same unlimited data call rates that home users get, or they should get untimed voice calls *to the Hip pocket nerve:* Another day, another rate hike for telecommunications users. What we want to know is why isn't the service being improved.

Emotive Language

Try to bring out expressions through your choice of words, and to strike a chord with the audience.

Example: Absolutely Disgusted with aanet ... Telstra has raised the signup fees Hence aaNet has had to surrender ! Is much more interesting than – " Telstra was absolutely disgusted by aanet and had to give in.

Inclusive Language

Try to be a part of the audience and make them feel connected to you. Include yourself in their group.

Example: " It's up to all of us to stand up to the multinational corporations whose rampant development is destroying our town" Is more convincing than " You should stand up to the multinational corporations whose rampant development is destroying the town."

Metaphors

A metaphor compares twp distinct things or objects without using the words "like or "as".

Example: "The former Governor-General, Sir William Deane, once referred to the ABS as providing a "mirror" on society. An appropriate metaphor, I'm sure you will agree.

Repetition

Repeat any particular word , usually the word which you need to bring in the notice of the audience and is the root cause of the problem.

Example: "House prices are up, fuel prices are up, grocery prices are up."

Rhetorical Question

It means a question that is asked just effect, without expecting any answer.

Example: "After the last fiasco, can the government really expect us to believe that they know what they're doing now?" Freely use some or all of the above mentioned tecniques to make your presentations more enaging.

Questions:

Asking a question right at the beginning of a presentation is a good way of letting your audience know that you wish to communicate *with* them, rather than simply lecture *at* them. It is your responsibility to make them feel comfortable during the session and to ensure that, you can start with some questions.

For the best effect, ask the audience a question that only allows for an unqualified 'Yes/No' answer (preferably 'Yes'), such as 'Can you hear me at the back?'

Also make sure that you are asking for a manageable response. The question: 'Is the seating comfortable?' is certainly relevant. But what do you do if a majority of the audience answer, 'No'?

Be careful while asking the questions, you should be able to acknowledge the audience response and do something about it! Suppose the audience is unable to hear you at the back, try to use a mike or to speak loudly. This way questions can act as a nice way to start the presentations.

Visual Impact

If you want people to take notice of what you have to say, dress as far as possible to meet your audience's expectations.

You could wait until everyone is seated, then leap on to the stage wearing a gorilla suit and waving a bunch of bananas. Or then again, maybe not.

Whilst fashions in general are becoming more relaxed, many people still believe that 'clothes make the man – or woman', and they will happily judge you on your physical appearance – and nothing else. The classic 'power outfit' for men is a dark suit, white shirt, a conservatively patterned tie with plenty of crimson or scarlet (not pillar box red!). Socks should be plain navy blue or black.

Shoes should be black, in good repair and well polished. (Judging a man by the state of his shoes is far more common in business circles than you might imagine.)

For women, changing attitudes mean that it is no longer necessary to wear a female version of the male power outfit described above. 'Classic' outfits, such as a blazer or collarless jacket with a skirt, trouser suits and dresses, are all acceptable.

Colour schemes should be sober (though not sombre), and chosen to complement individual hair, eye and skin coloration.

Items to avoid include lacy tops, floppy collars, conspicuous jewellery and scarves which need constant adjustment. You can use slight makeup but that should also be sober and not too prominent.

Example:

Lisha was asked to deliver a session introducing a research paper on which she had been working. It was an international conference, so she prepared her best, and confidently went to face the audience. She took the conference as an opportunity to represent her country and chose to wear a sari for the same. The moment she stepped on the stage, she suddenly felt uncomfortable. Everyone in the audience was dressed in western formals- mostly black suits. She had thought of representing her country by her dressing, but forgot the fact that she had never worn it before. As a result, she feared falling down while walking. The high heels made a sound each time she moved on the stage, and the open hair needed her constant attention. Offcourse, she ended the presentation, but by the end of it, nobody could get a hold of her session. She felt bad and decided to first inquire about the dress code at any such conferences and never experiment on the stage.

By the way, if the presentation is anything but a formal business event, is there any chance that people might be in doubt about what kind of clothes *they* should wear (formal business suit, smart casual or whatever)? It can save a lot of embarrassment if you specify the correct dress mode in the invitation to the presentation.

Whatever you wear, should be comfortable and you should not be conscious of your appearance all through the session.

Topical References

Topical references can be used to a great effect, as long as they are genuinely relevant to the subject under discussion – and everyone knows what you're talking about.

Shocking Statistics

If you want to use a shocking statistic – to get your audience's attention without actually insulting them – then make it as simple, but as hard-hitting as possible. Something like:

75 percent of all the retired people are living on a greatly reduced income. 30 percent of all the retired people are living on or below the poverty line.

[Short pause]

The material we're going to cover in this presentation could save you becoming a part of those statistics!

Used well, shocking statistics can be extremely effective, as long as you remember that statistics are easily misunderstood, unless the information is kept short and simple.

Outrageous Statements

Speaker (to the audience of computer programmers): 'Do you realise that you are wasting your time if you don't have a competent technical author to prepare your documentation!'

[Short pause]

'At least, that's how your customers may see it.'

From the audience's point of view, this was definitely a highly contentious opening, but it achieved its purpose.

The 'outrageous statement' opening will undoubtedly make your audience sit up and take notice, and if it (gently) ruffles a few feathers, it may also help the audience to remember the message when a more gentlemanly, neutral presentation has long since faded from memory.

Teasers

There was a particular trainer, who liked to have the following four instructions written up on a flipchart or whiteboard *before* the delegates started to arrive:

- ✓ Make mistakes. Ask 'dumb', questions, Cheat and have fun and Once the delegates were assembled, he would explain that the four points meant:
- ✓ Nobody is perfect, so understand that making mistakes is a valuable element in the learning process.
- ✓ If you don't understand something, say so, it's part of my job to make this as clear as I can.
- ✓ Forget everything you learnt in school about not looking at other people's work. In business, we work best when we pool our knowledge and our expertise.
- ✓ Treat this course as an *opportunity*, not as an obligation. The more you enjoy the course, the more effectively, you will absorb the course material.

Maps and Shoehorns

Once your audience is satisfactorily 'hooked', there are other functions, an introduction must serve.

In one situation, you may want to calm and reassure your audience, whilst on another occasion, it may be an essential part of the presentation that you get them stirred up and excited. In either case, one way of achieving the required result might be to 'draw a map' of the 'territory' you intend to cover in your presentation.

This is also an effective way of dealing with a situation where you know that different members of the audience have quite different views on the main topic of the presentation. In this case, the purpose of the 'mapping' process is to provide a clear, definitive view of the topic. You can't expect everyone to fall in line with your definition automatically, of course, but at least it will be plain to all concerned just where the presentation is coming from – and where you plan to go.

Just how detailed your map needs to be will depend on whether the members of your audience have any (relevant) prior knowledge of the topic being discussed. In some situations, people may have nearly as much information as you have yourself, in which case it is simply a question of fleshing out that knowledge so that they can make a decision, undertake a particular course of action, or whatever.

If you find that your audience knows little or nothing about the subject of the presentation, then your initial map must be more detailed than normal. But not so detailed that it becomes a summary of everything that you are going to talk about.

Think of it rather as a shoehorn, helping to ease the audience into the subject. Introduce some small part of your topic by relating it to something that the members of the audience will already know about and which matters to them. This will reassure them that your topic is comprehensible, and that the presentation is relevant to their current situation/ future needs. It will also give them the confidence to follow along, even if things get a little complicated and technical later on.

Various Types of Slides:
Text Slides

Text slides have one unbeatable advantage over more complex, graphic-driven slides: In terms of time they are really cheap. You can create a decent-looking text slide in a couple of minutes. These slides won't impress the audience much, but at least you will not be afraid you might forget what to say next.

Note: Don't, however, make a classical mistake of actually reading your slides to the audience aloud; there's nothing worse than that. Also, be very careful about the size of the font, it should be easily legible. What you really need for a text-based slide (moreso perhaps than for any other type of the slide) is focus. The biggest problem with text slides is that they are distracting. A little bit too much text and you can end up in trouble.

A presenter does not want people to read slides ahead of him. However, the good news is that people don't want to read slides. People don't even read documents anymore; they don't have time. Instead they try to quickly scan them to make sure they aren't missing anything important. So if you design your text slides for scanning rather than for reading, you will get more attention as a presenter.

Example:

Look at the Figure, which shows three slides from President Barack Obama's State of the Union address in 2011. This is the exact order in which they appear in the speech and they provide excellent support for the speech that an audience can easily scan.

What's the focal point of these slides?

It's in the centre, where the big numbers are. The rest of the slide is set in a noticeably smaller font. It is clear that "how much?" is the most important question here, and that the speaker is emphasising numbers with his words in his speech. Although, setting text in all capital letters reduces readability. It is probably okay for a short header, but not for the whole slide.

The figure shows an even shorter slide, which separates one part of the speech from another. Those kinds of slides are sometimes called 'bumper slides' because they act like a *buffer between different parts of the presentation.*

Lists

What's the text limit on a single slide? The figure below is a slide from Death by PowerPoint, trashing the once-classic 7×7 *rule*. The above template looks overcrowded with information and thus, should be avoided.

Seven is too much, but four is fine.

Now look at the next three text slides shown in the Figure. The first slide is not very imaginative but isn't bad either. It has a clear focal point in the header and clearly spaced bullet points underneath. We know what it's

Ditch stupid "rules"
- Do you remember the rule:
    - 7 lines per slide or less
    - 7 words per line or less?
- Well, it is just plain stupid
- If you follow this "rule"
- You get a slide like this

about the instant we see it. The template is good. The background is just a gradient blue; the white text is clearly visible; the header is set in a larger font. The second slide is much worse. First of all, it has the same header. If your next slide has the same header as the previous one, this is a signal that something is probably wrong. The audience loses the focus here. You knew where to look before for the main point; now you don't. The audience has to orient towards a new focal point, which will be the centre of the slide, where figures set in heavy type are. But the focus is not there. The numbers in the list don't make any sense before you move up and read the word, 'HELPED,' which is set in much thinner type. Also, the phrase, 'for less than 1%...' set in smaller type looks like a footnote. And footnotes have a really bad reputation; avoid them whenever possible.

Simple design rules*

1. **One** point per slide
2. **Few** matching colors
3. **Very** few fonts
4. **Photos**, not clipart

*pun intended

The third slide is a disaster. Its goal is to remind the audience of something that the speaker is mentioning only briefly. It is giving people a choice—to read or to listen. If they choose to read, they miss a part of the speech, and they cannot read it quickly enough, because there's too much text. They don't have time to digest this information.

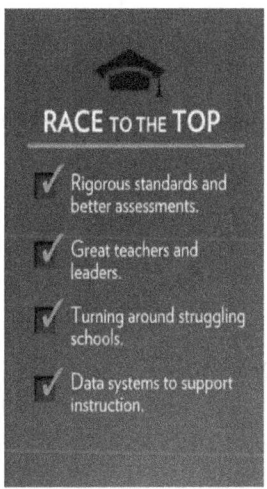 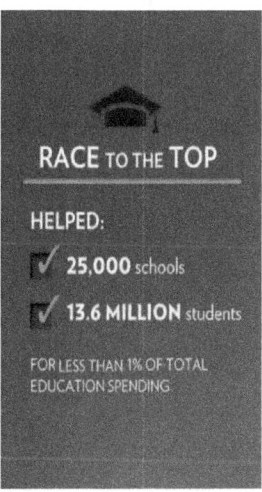 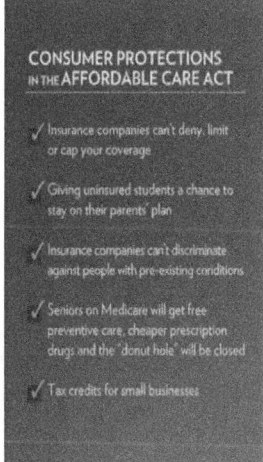

Bullets recently got a bad reputation. The purpose of the bullets is to create strong focal points so that you know where the next thought begins. This is especially helpful when scanning, when you don't read to the end of the sentence and jump right to the next sentence to see what's there. Unfortunately, the only situation when you need to jump like this is when you have a list, that is way too long.

Bullets actually do help; the top left slide is clearly better than the top right. However, if you take some time to think about what you are really trying to say, you can do it well without bullets. If your list has just four points, or you can pare it down to four points, then bullets bring no advantage.

If you have another strong focal point on your slide—such as a picture—you are better off without bullets. Clear spacing is essential for lists as the list takes all available space on a slide by adding extra space between paragraphs, versus cramming all the text in the upper part of the slide—as usually happens, if you just use default spacing.

Also, make sure your list has a clear order, with either the most important or the least important issues covered first. For Example, all the templates given below are followed for a presentation about Dogs. The last slide about dogs in the above figure goes with these spoken words: "Historically, dogs were mostly used for hunting and herding. Now their main roles are protection and, most importantly, companionship—which is what I am going to talk about." The dogs' roles on the slide are placed in historical order.

Dogs perform many roles:	Dogs perform many roles:
* Hunting	Hunting
* Herding	Herding
* Protection	Protection
* Companionship	Companionship
* Assisting police and military	Assisting police and military
* Aiding disabled individuals	Aiding disabled individuals

4 key roles for dogs:	4 key roles for dogs:
Hunting	 Hunting
Herding	Herding
Protection	Companionship
Companionship	Protection

Using Slides with Photos

The most elementary function of slides is to remind you what to say, and text slides do this very well. After you have finalized the text for the slides, the next stage is to decide if any additional parameters can be used to enhance the slides. Here we can choose from many supporting techniques and decide which messages need which kind of support. Illustrations, evidence and explanations are the three terms that help in making any slide more presentable. Illustrations provide emotional impact and retention.

Explanations explain.
Evidence proves.

Illustration is important when you need to add emotions in order to bring more life to your slides. You can ask the audience members to picture the dog in their mind's eye, or you can show them a picture of a dog and have a bigger impact.

Explanation helps if you want your audience to understand some complex, abstract idea, concept, or scheme.

If there's a trust issue between you and the audience, if they might not believe what you say, you need **evidence**. But remember that there's a notion in the legal profession called "the burden of proof."

This burden is two-fold; you make an effort to submit the evidence, while the audience makes an effort to process it. If you produce too much evidence, you will overload people with insubstantial details. If you don't produce enough evidence, your presentation will seem superficial and lack substance. So evidence is important, but not every slide is about evidence.

Using Illustrations:

A slide with a large photo and a short statement is an *archetypal Zen slide*. Photos are very powerful; they are a great way to reinforce your point and they don't take much time for the audience to process. There are just two challenges when using photos: finding them and combining them with your text.

Firstly, if you have your own photos—great. Nothing could be better. Using your own photographs shows that you care enough to take a picture for your audience to see. People appreciate that. Also, unlike stock photos, your photographs are authentic. They are really connected to the presentation, which is also appealing. We don't need to worry too much about the quality.

Photo quality was an issue several years ago, but now even pictures taken by cell phones look decent. Your audience's expectations about your artistic abilities aren't high. Just make sure the images are visible and they illustrate what you intend. There are so many photo editing software which are easy to learn and can be used to further enhance the picture, if needed.

Incase, you do not want to use your own photographs, as an alternate, there are many excellent websites selling photos or even offering free downloads. The problem is that it takes an enormous amount of time to find a suitable image. *Time just flies!* You look at the clock and see that you've just spent an hour and a half and found only two photographs out of the approximately 15 you need. Here are some hints to save you some time:

- ✓ At whatever stock photo site you are searching, type into the Search Box whatever you think, exactly how you think it. Don't try to rephrase it for the search algorithm, and don't be politically correct. What are you really trying to say? If you are looking for a secretary, ask for the secretary. This is very easy and sometimes it works.
- ✓ Try visualising in your mind's eye the picture you want and then 'describe' it to the Search Box. Be as specific as you can. If you see her as blond, search for 'blond.'
- ✓ If you have trouble visualising your ideas, use the Google image search instead of your mind's eye.

Warning: Never use images from a Google/Bing/Yahoo! image search. First, they are most likely to be copyrighted. Second, they are likely to be optimised for the Web, so quality will be an issue.

It is quite easy to illustrate concrete ideas like events, places, or actions. It's hard to illustrate abstract concepts like trust or values, and this is where illustrations are especially powerful. If you have trouble visualising abstract ideas, tell Google what you need. If you like some of the pictures, you see, 'describe' them to a stock photography website. Determine how people solved this problem before on Google, and if you like one you find, just create an image more or less the same.

However, the biggest problem with stock imagery is that people produce pictures that they want to sell. How exactly is this a problem? If you want to sell a photo, it has to illustrate some behaviour, emotion, or concept that frequently occurs in life— essentially, a stereotype. *Stock photography is stereotypical.* People sell clichés; that's their business. You're probably seeing those images in every other presentation: a handshake, a blue globe, stacks of coins, hands holding sprouting trees, unbelievably diverse teams with members of every race, age group, gender and sexual orientation.

Although there's nothing wrong with illustrating a concept of a car with a picture of a car. The problem with such cliché images is that they do not represent the concerned emotion authentically. The problem with the handshake is *not* that it's not original; it's that it is not authentic, it's fake. It doesn't really represent partnership. Partnership maybe starts with a handshake, but it's not a handshake. Shaking hands doesn't automatically make people partners.

It really depends on the context. Now if you take time and think what makes people partners in your case and illustrate that, it will be a great illustration.

Using Abstract Illustrations

If you need to explain rather than to impress, there are different types of images for that. Have a look at the figure below. The first picture is a photograph of a man wearing a uniform and smiling. This is an actual person with a name. His face produces an emotional response. We might like it or not.

The next picture is much more abstract. It may even represent the same person, but a lot of details are gone. There are no facial expressions to interpret; this person is more generic and replaceable. It's not a person anymore; it represents the workforce. Far fewer emotions are engaged by this illustration. However, you can still see his hairstyle, a badge, and his basic shape. The last picture is as abstract as it gets. It's not entirely clear whether this is a male or female.

Sometimes less emotion is what you need. If you need to illustrate a process, draw a map, show relationships, or explain an abstract concept, photos aren't the best way to go. Instead, use *pictograms,* *contours* and *geometric shapes.* The visual language helps to resolve the serious problem of information overload.

Tailor It

Clip arts, Pictograms and Process Charts:

Apart from the images, you can also use *clip arts, pictograms* or *process charts* for illustration. There is, however, an important difference: You use them for concepts rather than for actual events or people. Clip art, in a **graphic art**, and refers to pre-made images used to illustrate any medium.

Pictography is a form of **writing** which uses representational and pictorial **drawings**. Pictographs are often used in writing and graphic systems in which the characters are to a considerable extent pictorial in appearance. The *flow process chart in* **industrial engineering** is a graphical and **symbolic representation** of the **processing** activities performed on the work piece.

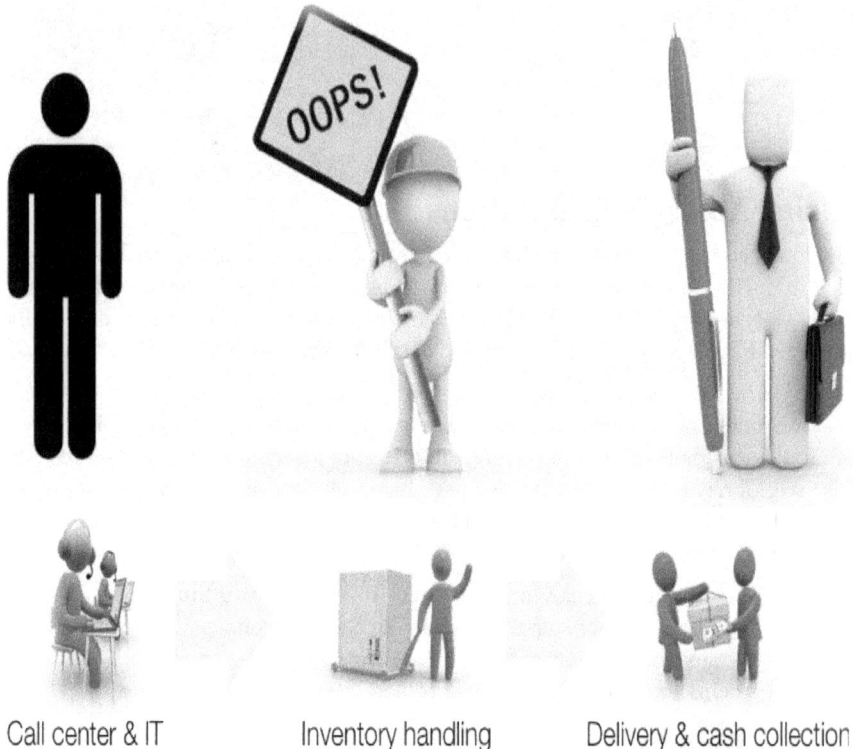

Call center & IT   Inventory handling   Delivery & cash collection

Figure below shows some of President Barack Obama's slides again. The first slide's focus is on the $1,000 figure, but in the background, we see a silhouette of a family receiving those benefits. It would be a mistake to use the photograph as the focus because it's not a particular family; it's an abstract family, and hence the abstract picture.

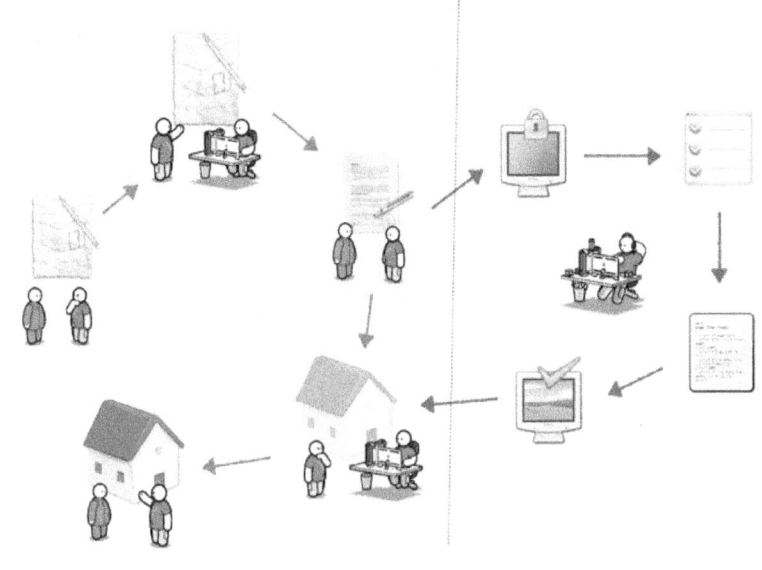

On the next slide, the emphasis is on the figure, '$630 per year'—it's bright orange—as well as on the plug and the thunderbolt representing electricity. The last slide is a mistake because this is where they could have shown a photograph of the school. It doesn't because this is where they could have shown a photograph of the school. It doesn't matter that much where it is located, and seeing actual students who had improved their reading scores would be more effective.

To Summarise

Illustrate actual ideas or events. Don't insert pictures just because using pictures looks good.'

Use pictures to highlight. Pictures carry a powerful emotional charge. Don't let that go to waste. Use pictures to evoke emotion and to motivate, also to attract readers in the beginning and in the end. The middle is more about explanations.

What's the most important point of your picture? Does it display what you are trying to say? Make sure your picture is cropped so that important points are big enough.

 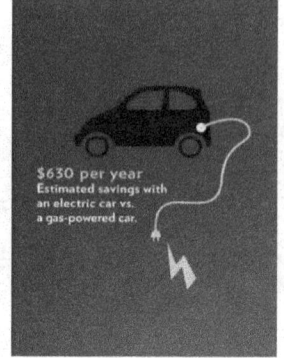 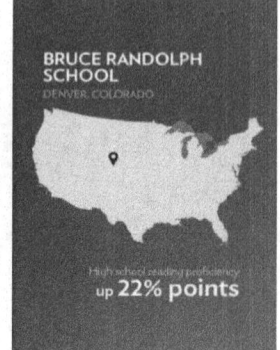

Chapter 6

Everyone has a different way of remembering what they have to say. Whatever technique you use, ensure that it is effective. You do not, need to memorise a presentation, word by word. If you are done with your preparation then it should be your ability to add value to content that the audience wants to hear and not what you can memorise like a script. Also, memorising your presentation, word by word will make it sound unnatural and you run into the risk of forgetting one word or other which will affect the entire presentation.

We agree, reading your presentation is suitable in some cases like reading a testimonial on someone's life or while delivering a speech where it is important that you do not miss a quote. For all the other presentations conducted every day, your goal should be to hold the audience's attention to a maximum level and reading to them will likely put them to sleep. The best way to deliver a presentation is to use your own words. A presentation is a sequence of thoughts; if the thoughts are out of sequence, the presentation won't make much sense. The best way to remember a presentation is to use key phrases and rehearse.

1. Key Phrases

If you are going to deliver a long presentation, type it word by word – it doesn't need to be perfect though. Now go through it and divide it further into naturally occurring parts and sub-parts. Your initial structure may provide sufficient division but if required you may need to divide it further. This will be applicable only to the body of the presentation, as the beginning and the end may be worth memorising.

Wherever appropriate, type in very short phrases that reflect the point you are trying to make in that part. You know you have done this correctly if you were to read these phrases sequentially and they have encapsulated your entire presentation. These are the phrases you need to remember. You don't say the phrases they are just there to guide you.

2. Rehearsal

In addition to using the key phrases you must rehearse your presentation, irrespective of whether it is an elevator pitch or a long presentation. **Here are few tips for rehearsal:**

- ✓ Plan to rehearse your presentation loud and against the clock at least four times. What your presentation sounds like when you self-talk is not what it sounds like when you say it out loud.
- ✓ For low level presentations, at least rehearse out loud once in the car or in the shower or at your desk, wherever you can.
- ✓ For high level presentations, in addition to couple of normal rehearsals, also rehearse in the venue or location and with the whole team if possible.
- ✓ Plan the choreography – who will be moving where and when. This will also include planning the seating of the audience and of your team.
- ✓ Include others when rehearsing and get their feedback.

The benefits of a well documented rehearsal are:

- ✓ It decreased anxiety and you feel better.
- ✓ You sound better when you rehearse well.
- ✓ You feel more prepared as you get to hear how convincing you are.

Your rehearsal(s) for a presentation should be part of the process of preparing your script. Once you have drafted the outline of your script, put it on audio tape, (videotape is even better) and then run it through with the following thoughts in mind:

- ✓ Does your presentation follow a clear sequence of ideas?
- ✓ Have you aimed the material at the right level?
- ✓ Have you included material that isn't strictly relevant?
- ✓ Are you trying to cover too much information?
- ✓ How and where can you use visual aids to clarify and enhance the basic presentation?
- ✓ Are you presenting your material in an appropriate manner?

Armed with the answers to these questions, and any others which seem important to you, work your first draft into something more precise. By the way, rehearsals are especially important when a presentation is to be a team project. Even if all the members of the team are experienced presenters, at least one team rehearsal is necessary:

- ✓ To make sure that 'handing on the baton' goes smoothly at each change of the presenter.
- ✓ To check the timing of each section of the presentation.
- ✓ To check the material – it is not unknown (when rehearsals don't take place) for one member of the team to stray beyond the topic assigned to them and thus, pre-empt the comments planned by a later speaker.

- ✓ To ensure that the presentation has the appearance of a well co-ordinated production.

Many people attending a team presentation, especially potential customers, will place quite a lot of importance on how well the presenters work together *as a team*. Rightly or wrongly, members of the audience may assume that the ability of the team members to work together – or not – is an indication of how well their company works in general.

Handle the Situation

You're sitting quietly at your desk when suddenly a call comes: "We need a presentation, and only you can do it Riya!" How do you feel? Proud? Cautious? Or do you just PANIC? Since most people are likely to opt for panic, why not use this as your advantage. Let us see the key elements of a good presentation:

- ✓ Outline your Purpose
- ✓ Analyse your Audience
- ✓ Identify the Need
- ✓ Collate your Information
- ✓ Prepare your Communication

Did you notice something? Probably you don't Check it out again:

- ✓ Outline your **P**urpose
- ✓ **A**nalyse your **A**udience
- ✓ Identify the **N**eed
- ✓ Collate your **I**nformation
- ✓ Prepare your **C**ommunication

Yes, it forms the word, PANIC. Let us discuss all these elements one by one.

Purpose

In many cases, the purpose of a presentation will not be a matter of choice. It will probably be dictated to you by someone else:

- ✓ Your department head asks you to show Gaurav Khurana(a new employee) the ropes.
- ✓ You are chosen to give the senior management a brief overview of the work done by your team.
- ✓ It is your task to carry out the proceedings at a sales conference in a positive and motivating way.

In order to produce a successful presentation, you must have a clear idea of what the presentation is to be about. Also, your understanding must be both short and accurate. If required, gather further information until you are sure that you have a solid hold on that purpose:

- ✓ Are you required to train Gaurav Khurana in some specific tasks, or simply you need to familiarise him with the general routine?
- ✓ Will you be giving a solo presentation to the senior management, or will you be one of the few speakers?
- ✓ What are the current sales figures like? Will your own presentation be preceded by rewards or recriminations?

There has been many a good presentation that has fallen by the wayside because the speaker wasn't sufficiently clear about his/her purpose.

Audience

In the examples, we have mentioned, a specific audience that has been mentioned each time – the new employee, senior management and the sales team. One of the first things, you should do when preparing for any presentation is to find out as much as you can about your audience. Even if you don't get an opportunity to meet any of the members from your audience in advance, you can still use a simple but powerful test to make a pretty accurate estimate.

Question 1: If I'm describing a new idea to you, would you prefer that I start with:

(a) the details, or

(b) the big picture?

Question 2a: If you answered (a) to question 1, would you like me to:

(c) work up from the details to the bigger picture, or

(d) stick with the details?

Question 2b: If you answered (b) to question 1, would you want me to

(e) work down to a more detailed description, or

(f) stick with the big picture?

If you answered (a) and (d), you obviously prefer to work with details available, whereas someone who selected (b) and (f) is probably much more comfortable dealing in general information. A person who selects (a) and (c) is mainly detail-oriented, but is also interested to see how those details are related to the big picture. Finally, if you selected (b) and (e), then you probably prefer to work in with general information, but also being able to deal with more precise details when that is appropriate. We can apply these conclusions to job roles to estimate what kind of presentation style the corresponding job-holders might prefer.

Most senior managers and board members are required to think in terms of company strategy for the next five years, and competition at the national and international level. It seems likely, then, that such people would select answers (b) and limited (e) – indicating a fairly non-detailed type of presentation.

Staff of the R&D department is more likely to answer (a) and (d), which would call for lots of facts and figures in either the presentation or the handout. A presentation at a Sales Conference might tend to be (b) and (f) if the main purpose is to celebrate the year's results, or (b) and very limited (e) at the rollout of a new product.

Need

Every presentation has a purpose, and answers a need or needs. The purpose of taking Gaurav Khurana through the office procedures may be to bring him up to speed in his job as quickly as possible, but what are his needs? Does he need detailed instructions, or just a brief info? And what do you need in order to be able to meet this requirement? Do you need to do some research? Is this a routine situation for you, or it is a chance to put yourself in line for promotion?

The more clearly you can define the needs of the situation, the more chance you have of giving a really good and focussed presentation.

Information

So, you now know who your presentation is for, and why. But what information should be included to achieve the required outcome? If you give too little information, the event becomes a waste of everyone's time. Give too much information and most of it will be forgotten by the next day.

The more accurately you define your goal, the easier it will be to determine what must go into the presentation – and what can be left out.

Communication

What visual aids will you use (if any)? Where will the presentation taken place? What kind of follow-up will be required? This is where you plan the framework for your presentation, and consider the all-important question: How will it be perceived by your audience (will they hear what you meant to say, what you did say, what they think you said or what they think you meant by what they think they heard you say)?

Importance of FOCUS

An effective way to acquire new skills is to find out what well - known experts do, understand and what makes them successful, and then apply that behaviour in your own life. Let us list the skills most frequently used by people who are rated by their colleagues as outstanding presenters:

- ✓ Fine-tuning
- ✓ Outcome-oriented
- ✓ Chunking
- ✓ Unlimited points of view
- ✓ Success assurance

So did you notice something special here. Probably, you missed it again. Let us check out the list again:

- ✓ Fine-tuning

- ✓ Outcome-oriented
- ✓ Chunking
- ✓ Unlimited points of view
- ✓ Success assurance

Yes, that gives us **FOCUS**. Let us discuss the importance of these factors one by one.

Fine-tuning

A skilled presenter constantly refines his material to make it as appropriate as possible for a given audience. This process continues until the very end of the event, and the presenter will repeatedly check that the presentation is headed in the right direction, using his skill and flexibility to adapt the *style, tempo* and *focus* of the presentation in order to achieve his/her original objectives.

Achieving Outcome

If you don't know where you want to go, how will you know which route to take? And how will you know when you've arrived? Top presenters work to answer two basic questions right from the start of the planning stage:

- ✓ What do I want the presentation to achieve?
- ✓ How will the audience behave if I am achieving my outcome?

Effective Chunking

Chunking is the process of presenting information in manageable segments. Some people like to begin with an overview and work down the lane, and others will prefer to start with the details and build up to the details. Skilled presenters most frequently begin with an overview and work down to the details.

Unlimited Points of View

Many top speakers give their presentations from three different positions: Position 1 is their own viewpoint, Position 2 is the audience's viewpoint, and Position 3 is the neutral observer position.

By mentally switching from one position to another, they can give their presentation a personal dimension (in Position 1), they can judge how they are coming across to the audience (in Position 2), and they can avoid any conflict or confrontation, should it arise (by moving to Position 3).

This particular skill takes time to develop, but it is an amazingly effective key for handling any kind of audience and any kind of situation.

Success Assurance

The fifth characteristic common to most of the skilful presenters is a self-belief that each presentation is bound to be successful, no matter what happens. - IT CAN BE DONE!

Please understand that visualisation wont work in the cases where you try to convince yourself about something which you don't really believe is possible. For the best results, set yourself realistic goals and build upon them as your belief grows.

Tell yourself that you are going to do the best job you can on this presentation, that you are going to be successful, and that you deserve that success. If it is at all possible, do take the opportunity to get the feel of the room (where the presentation will take place) – its size, effect of any background noise, the seating layout, etc.

Focus your attention on positive images around (if any) and feel positive about your role in the presentation. If the whole visualisation process seems a bit strange at first, not to worry, just go with it, this is perfectly normal and it won't prevent you from achieving a beneficial result. After only a few days, you will begin to notice changes in your attitude towards the presentation.

Pictures and Images

What role does pictures and images play in a presentation? They play quite a significant role actually. Before reading this section, please close your eyes and imagine relaxing on a beautiful beach in Goa. Take particular note of the first thing that comes to mind.

So, what was that first thought? Was it a picture of gentle waves on the sea or of a clear blue sky or something else? Or was it a sound of waves splashing gently on the shore, perhaps? Or was it a feeling of fine sand beneath your feet for example?

If the first thought was some kind of picture then your primary thinking style (we will call it PTS) in this context is visual(based on images). If your first thought was of something you could hear, then your PTS for this experience is auditory(based on audio). And if your first thought was about how you felt (physically or emotionally), then your PTS is kind of aesthetic.

In the above examples, we have at times imagined the images, so you should be clear to the fact that visualisation is not only limited to pictures, but also to mental images.

Some Tips on How to Create Confidence

In addition to building confidence through being well prepared and through understanding your audience, there are also ways of directly installing and boosting your own level of confidence.

Relaxation

Firstly, a *simple relaxation technique*. For best results take a relaxation break every day:

1. Find somewhere quiet where you can be free of disturbances for 10–20 minutes (10 minutes is OK, 20 minutes is more than twice as effective).

2. All you need is a comfortable seat, preferably with arm rests, but not so comfortable that you will be tempted to fall asleep.
3. At a convenient time (more or less the same time each day is preferable, but not essential) go to this quiet place and sit in the chair with your arms on the arm rests and legs slightly apart.
4. Close your eyes and take a minute or two to get used to any of the little noises that may occur.
5. When you are ready, start to pay attention to your breathing by counting from 1 to 10 – breathe in (1), breathe out (2), breathe in (3) and so on. When you get to 10, start again from 1.

Not only is this process beneficial to your overall health, it has the added advantage that, after a few sessions, doing it for just two or three minutes shortly before a presentation is enough to put you in a calm and resourceful state.

The Circle of Excellence

The second technique is generally known as 'the circle of excellence', and is incredibly effective. You can do it on your own if you wish, though many people find it easier if they have someone to read the instructions to them:

1. Find a quiet place where you will not be overlooked or disturbed for about 5–10 minutes.
2. Decide exactly what 'state' you want to install – *calmness, confidence, feeling motivated* and so on.
3. Stand somewhere in the middle of this space in a comfortable pose and gently shake both arms, then each leg in turn, just to loosen up and 'break state', as it's sometimes called.
4. Imagine that there is a circle on the floor in front of you about 1 metre (3 feet) across. You don't need to be able to visualise it – just be comfortable with the idea that it is there.
5. Then imagine that it is filled with your favourite colour.
6. With your eyes open or shut, whichever you prefer, imagine a relevant situation and what it would be like if you were in exactly the state you want to be in. Think of how you would like to feel and what you might be seeing and hearing. If you can actually recall a previous experience of being in the desired state – in this case being confident– so much the better. The more vividly we imagine an event, the more readily the brain will 'remember' it as though it actually happened.
7. Think of an appropriate word or a short phrase, such as 'Now' or 'I'm ready.'

8. When the memory seems to be reaching full strength, step forward into the circle, whilst repeating your 'trigger' – under your breath, of course.
9. As the feeling begins to fade, if you have your eyes closed, open them. Remember the experience for a moment or two, then step out of the circle and do the short 'break state' exercise (see Step 3).
10. Rerun the process several times. You will normally find that by the second or third repeat, you can simply step into the circle and the feeling of confidence will kick in more or less automatically with little or no conscious effort on your part.

All you have to do when it comes to the actual event is to imagine the coloured circle in front of you and then step into it, whilst saying the 'trigger'. Then deliver your presentation with confidence.

Relax Your Mind:

The best state to be in just before you give a presentation is relaxed but alert. This may depend on whether you are a 'day person' or a 'night person'.

Day people find it easy to make an early start, but they tend to run out of steam later in the day. Night people, by contrast, may find it quite hard going to handle early morning sessions, and will be far more lively in the afternoon. If you are a night person, and you have to give a presentation in the early morning, set the alarm at least a half-hour earlier than usual.

This will give your body enough time to get into gear before you step into the spotlight. For relaxation, on the other hand, you might like to consider listening to a tape of violin music by Mozart or one of the baroque composers (Vivaldi, Handel, etc), which is restful without causing drowsiness.

Practise Voice Modulation:

When you first begin to give presentations, you might also want to set the microphone a little way away from you so that you can learn to project your voice. There are two main points of difference between *projecting* your voice and *raising* your voice (the latter is technically referred to as shouting):

1(a) To project your voice, you must use your *diaphragm* to drive the air up through your throat and mouth.

1(b) When you shout, you use your *neck muscles* to do all the work.

2(a) When you project your voice, you should find that you can talk as easily as if you were conversing with someone only a short distance away. Projecting your voice should not cause any kind of physical strain.

2(b) When you shout, it *hurts*!

If you have trouble learning to project your voice correctly, you may find that it is worth paying a couple of visits to a *professional voice coach or singing teacher*.

Finally, when you feel that you've got things almost right – stop rehearsing. To give a really good performance, you must have as much interest in your presentation as you want to see in your audience, and that's not very likely if you've already rehearsed it to death.

Chapter 7

Importance of Delivery

If you want to effectively communicate with your audience, to *influence, persuade or just create a good impression*, you need to adapt your delivery style to match the expectations and communication needs of your audience. This is about increasing the size of your delivery skill toolbox, so you can use the right tool for the job. This takes work and practice but the good news is your tool box is different to everyone else's. So your version of dynamic voice will be different to everyone else's, and your version of 'serious' is also different to everyone else's. But here's the thing, the audience knows if you are faking.

Watch videos of people who do it well, try and emulate that facet and make it your own. Please note that we are not saying copy other people, but observe them and learn and see how you can incorporate that element into your style. This may be such things as noticing how a presenter may smile a lot or pause or emphasise with a subtle gesture.

There are two types of presentations; Presentations that are made to large groups of people that you see CEO's, politicians and VIP's give which are when done well, these are the ones you typically and unfairly think you need to emulate. The second type of presentation is the one you give every day to colleagues, clients and at social gatherings. In these situations, don't feel you have to present like your favourite politician. You have to present the best you can and your style of delivery will depend on four things:

Subject: What you are there to talk about?

Occasion: This is a product launch, conference or birthday speech.

Audience: Think about their expectations, communication styles, motivations and titles.

Your Personality: Don't try and be someone you are not, just be the best you can be.

Content Delivery   97

The following figure shows the Key success factors according to Estrada et al.

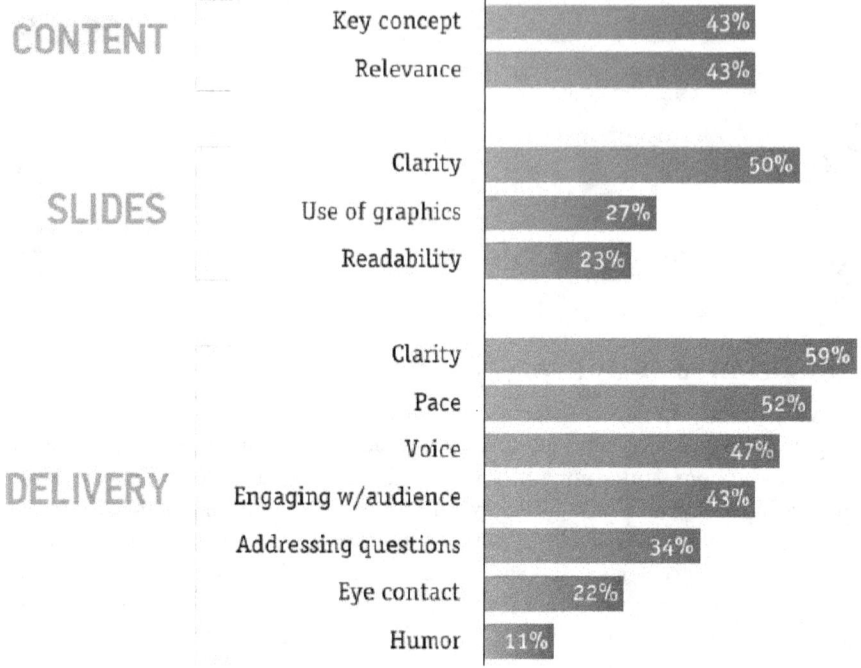

So let us have a look at the different behaviours and then ask ourselves, what you need to work on.

1. Behaviours

Facial Expression

Smiling is a powerful cue that transmits friendliness, warmth and approachability. Smiling is often contagious and others will react favourably. They will be more comfortable around you and more open to the information you are offering.

Eye Contact

Steady eye contact helps to regulate the flow of communication, encourages participation, and can be used to develop rapport with the audience. When the audience feels that you see them as individuals, they are more likely to trust you and be more open to your recommendations. Some tips for using eye contact to build rapport include:

> ✓ **Length of Eye Contact:** Try to maintain an eye contact with one person at a time for at least 3 – 5 seconds or until you complete a thought. This helps to establish a connection with people and helps you to avoid darting eyes, which can be distracting and communicate nervousness.

- ✓ *Movement of Eyes:* Direct eye contact towards different parts of the audience throughout the course of your presentation. Staring too long in one direction may cause you to miss important information and can make certain audience members feel less important.
- ✓ *Search for Friendly Eyes:* If you are nervous, look for a friendly audience member and establish eye contact with that person.

Some Habits to Avoid Include:

- ✓ *Talking to the Ceiling:* Don't present to a spot over the tops of the audience's heads. They may think you don't care or they may feel that you are "above them."
- ✓ *Talking to the Screen:* Don't speak to your notes, to the whiteboard, or to your visuals.
- ✓ *Clutching Your Notes:* Be familiar with your material. Being tied to your notes or a manual keeps you from establishing eye contact and may cause the audience to question your knowledge, preparedness, and confidence.

When presenting to groups you need to have stronger eye contact than usual. Have you ever been to a concert and thought the performer was looking directly at you? Maybe they were, maybe not – either way they were using a technique called clustering. In this technique you group the audience into clusters. If you have a large audience your clusters are very small in the first row - one or two people and the cluster becomes bigger the further you go back. If it's a very large audience then the clusters may be as big as twenty people toward the back.

Now target an individual in each cluster, and hold eye contact with that person as you deliver a thought or idea. When focusing on the clusters at the front of the room hold for a duration of 4 -5 seconds and when focusing on clusters at the back hold for up to 10 seconds. Move randomly amongst the clusters. This gives the impression that you are looking at everyone in the cluster.

Next figure demonstrates an average person's field of view. This is how wide you can see without turning your head. The actual field is even smaller; most of it in any given moment is peripheral vision, which is good only for recognizing motion and well-known patterns.

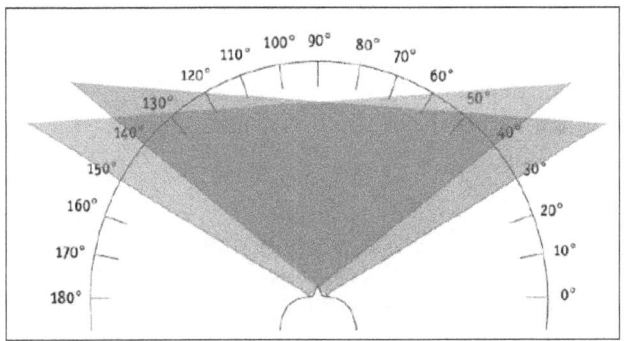

The next figure shows an overhead view of a presentation space with 20 people. If you stand like this, you will get very good contact with people right in front of you, some contact with people on the periphery, and very little contact with people sitting too far (depending on how well you see) and in the corners. This is no good.

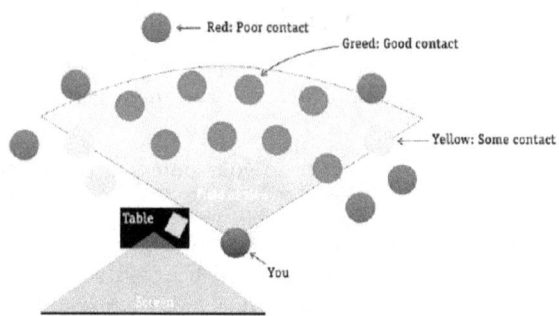

If possible, ask people to move closer to each other in front of you, so that you can see them all without turning your head much.

Posture

You communicate numerous messages by the way you hold yourself, while presenting. A person who is slouching or leaning with arms across their chest may be perceived as being uninterested or unapproachable. Standing erect, facing the audience with an open stance, and leaning forward communicates that you are receptive and friendly. Speaking with your back turned or looking at the floor or ceiling should be avoided as it communicates disinterest.

Body Movement

Moving naturally around a room or stage increases interaction, adds interest, and draws attention to the presentation. Staying frozen in the front of the room can be distracting and boring for people to watch. Shuffling feet and pacing can convey nervousness and lack of confidence.

Gestures

A lively speaking style captures attention, makes the material more interesting, and facilitates understanding. Use natural movements to emphasise topics and free, easy arm and hand movements to add personality to your presentation. If you fail to gesture while speaking, you may be perceived as boring and stiff.

Proximity

Cultural norms dictate a comfortable distance for interaction with others. When interacting, a presenter needs to be aware of people's defined levels of personal space. Do not invade an audience member's intimate space. Most adults will feel uncomfortable, even if a rapport has been established.

Voice

Voice is another area of communication that can affect the quality of audience retention. An interesting and audible voice will be engaging, while a soft or monotone voice can cause boredom or disinterest among participants. While it may be difficult to listen to and change your own voice, with awareness and practice, it is possible to use one's voice effectively. The first step to refining your voice is to understand the components of voice and identify the common voice problems. Once identified, most voice problems can be improved by being aware of the problem, altering some habits, and practising new behaviours on a regular basis.

Pace

Pace is how long a sound lasts. Talking too fast causes words and syllables to be short, while talking slowly lengthens them. Varying pace helps to maintain the audience's interest. If you are continuously talking too fast or too slow:

- ✓ Be aware of your normal conversational pace and keep in mind how tension affects the speed in which you talk,
- ✓ Use breathing and natural pauses to slow down your pace, and constantly vary your pace in order to maintain the audience's interest.

Projection

Projection is directing the voice so that it can be plainly heard at a distance. Problems with projection are often the result of tension, breathiness and breathing from your throat. Try to avoid projecting from your throat which can lead to sore throats, coughing, and loss of your voice. Take slow, deep breaths, initiated from your abdomen. Open your mouth fully and speak to the people in the back of the room.

Articulation

Articulation is the ability to pronounce words distinctly. It often reflects your attitude towards the words you are speaking. Clear enunciation reflects self-confidence and interest, while slurred or mumbled speech, indicate insecurity or indifference. To remedy this, speak at a slower pace than your normal conversational tone, take the time to pronounce each letter or sound within a word and listen for common articulation problems, such as dropping the "g" at the end of words, such as finding or going.

Pitch

Pitch is the normal range of the voice – *its highness or lowness*. Everyone is capable of a wide voice range. Stress and poor breathing can greatly alter the pitch of your voice. Try to adjust your pitch to convey different meanings throughout a presentation. To alter pitch, control your breathing; breathe from your abdomen and slow your rate of speech, take pauses to relax between pitch changes.

Inflection

Inflection is the manner in which the pitch varies as you speak. Inflection serves as *verbal punctuation* and involves *changing pitch* to convey meaning. Upward inflections ask a question, suggest uncertainty or doubt, and communicate hesitancy. Downward inflections give information and convey strength and authority to the audience. Use upward and downward inflections appropriately. Avoid constant middle inflection where the voice neither rises nor falls, but just drones on and on. *Each event, meeting or interaction, you have has a different setting and combination.* So if you have only one setting in every presentation, better be exactly the same.

2. Nerves

Feeling nervous is a good thing (just not too nervous). Now, have a look at the chart given below.

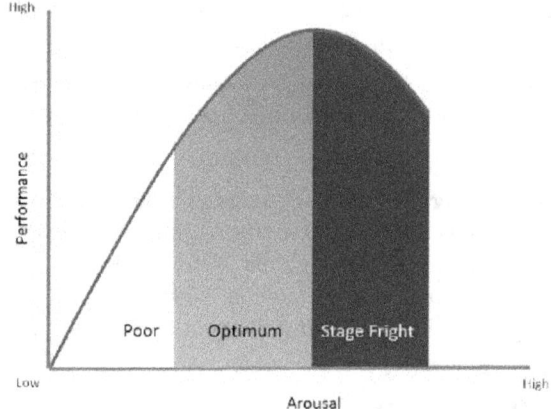

The *Yerkes-Dodson* law demonstrates an *empirical relationship between arousal and performance.* It dictates that performance increases with cognitive arousal, but only to a certain point: when levels of arousal become too high, performance will decrease.

When you present, you want to be in the grey zone, here your arousal or adrenalin is at the right level. If you substitute the word arousal for fear, you can conclude that a certain amount of fear is a good thing – too much is what we call stage fright where you stutter, stumble and sweat your way through a presentation. So if you suffer from stage fight, the trick is not to eradicate what you are feeling but to 'knock the edge off'. So you move into the grey zone. Think of it like an athlete – if they are not pumped before going onto the field (in the grey zone) they won't perform at their peak. Too much adrenaline and they could perform poorly.

Ted Schredd has written a great article on the *physiological similarities between fear and excitement.* Here is a piece of great advice:

Most of your fears are imagined and should be treated as *imaginary*. Learn to distinguish the fears that are valid and those that are not. The next time you feel scared, challenge your fear and the thing you fear will disappear. Ask yourself, "What would I do if I wasn't feeling fearful?" Then act accordingly. When you confront your fears, astonishing things will happen. Remember, you are the master and you are in control.

The second thing we want to talk about is the importance of content and delivery. Many presenters put undue pressure on themselves because they believe they don't deliver well and as a consequence build up unbelievable levels of anxiety. Remember, if you get your content right using a solid strategy, the delivery will begin to take care of itself. You will come across as being confident, authentic and believable – your audience will sense this and will complement you accordingly. I'm not saying that delivery is not important; *you just have to get the order right – content first then work on your delivery.*

Some communication consultants site studies, such as Albert Mehrabian's work which states that the meaning of a message is communicated by:

Your words -7%

Your tone of voice-38%

Your body language-55%

They then use this information to tell you that delivery is the only thing that matters.

3. Answering Questions

When answering questions, don't be afraid to take your time and understand the question. So it can be answered properly. Use these steps and structure your answer.

- ✓ Listen: Focus on the person asking the question and focus on them.
- ✓ Clarify: After listening to the question, if necessary, articulate back your understanding of the subject matter.
- ✓ Paraphrase: Then paraphrase back your understanding of the question.
- ✓ Decide: Decide whether you have sufficient information on hand to answer the question – so this is a 'yes' or 'no' situation.
- ✓ Respond: Either say you will respond later or give your answer.

4. Logistics

Timing – Presenting Time *vs.* Q&A Time

If you have a group of people presenting and you have an hour, a typical split may be *15 minutes question time* and *35 minutes presenting time*. The ten minutes buffer is for late starts and more questions. If it's just you presenting a just look to cut the buffer down.

Presenting Environment

For important or major presentations, always check the venue. Check the following:

- ✓ *Equipment* – Does it work and do you know how to use it.
- ✓ *Venue location* – Give yourself time to get there and make sure you are early
- ✓ *Seating* - How is it organised; theatre, boardroom or u-shaped, and does it need to be changed
- ✓ *Plan your movement* – Can you move or are you stuck in one place
- ✓ *Do a full rehearsal* in the venue if you can
- ✓ *Check the lighting* – If there is a lot of natural light, check that it doesn't wash out any projected images.

One final point on this: When you present, remember that the space is yours – if there is something in your way move it, or something not working, change it. You've done too much work to be brought undone at the last minute.

Best Type of Visual Aids

Assess and know how to use the best type of visual aids for the environment. You should be mindful of the visual aids, you are using and the environment. Some years ago, a confectionary company was holding a product launch for an aeronautically themed chocolate. They held the launch in an airport hangar – which was a great idea. The only problem was that when the doors on the hanger were open, the projection screen was totally washed out. In addition, don't over-compensate by making the room as dark as possible, so dark that you can't see your audience.

Are Additional Notes Necessary?

If you are going to have handouts, be conscious of when you are going to distribute these. Here are some for and against statements for using handouts.

At the Beginning

For: Well laid out, they can be highly effective, one or two pages are ideal.

Against: If there are too many pages, the audience may be distracted by them and not listen to you.

During

For: One page at a time retains control.

Against: Frustrating for some audiences.

At the End

For: If additional information is required – This can be useful.

Against: Environmentally unfriendly – Email may be a better option.

At the Door on the Way Out
For: Only those who require a copy will take one.

Against: They may not take them and once again environmentally unfriendly.

Expectations of the Audience
Look carefully at the audience and clearly understand their expectations. If your audience is expecting all the bells and whistles, then give it to them. If they want a conversation, then ditch the visual aids and the formalities. If you are not going to give the audience what they expect, then let them know in advance. If you are there to entertain your audience, then the element of surprise is yours.

5. Visual Aids of the Audience
Presenting in a business context is about influencing or persuading an audience. From a visual aids perspective this means that everything you use must enhance the audiences understanding of the topic. So when you are crafting your visual aids think about the audience needs first, not yours.

Here are Some Guiding Principles for Thinking about Visual Aids;
- ✓ Don't project text and talk to it, because people can either listen to you or read, they can't do both.
- ✓ Hand out as much information as possible, organise it on as few pages as possible (preferably 1 page), put it into some form of sequential flow so that people can follow your logic, and include as much relevant quantitative detail as possible.
- ✓ Do project relevant high resolution graphics and talk about them. Also, incorporate a little explanatory text.
- ✓ Leave out unimportant material.
- ✓ Incorporate video clips, if relevant.
- ✓ Don't use clip art.

Handling a Discussion
Starting a discussion with the audience is really easy. All you need to do is to cease censoring yourself. You need to get moderately angry at something that relates to them, maybe with somebody else who closely resemble your audience, maybe, with some particular person in the group.

Handling the Expert in the Crowd:

Sometimes, you will encounter an expert in your audience. Presentations are a very broad field. So we often encounter somebody with much more experience in scriptwriting, for example. We tend to avoid discussions with experts. Yes, we are concerned about our reputation, but this is not the main reason. The problem with experts in a group setting is that they speak in their own language, which is often incomprehensible to the rest of the group. Pretty soon, it becomes a discussion just between the two parties.

Believe us, we have tried to have those discussions, but terms and names start flying around that nobody else knows or cares about. So, when we hear the second very specific question or objection from the same person, we just say, "Apart from you and me, nobody else understands this question, right?" I look at the audience. They nod. "I am very sorry, but your questions are overly specific. We cannot afford a private discussion at the expense of everybody else; do you agree? Could you please write your questions down so that we can discuss them later?"

If the question is well formulated and the audience really cares, we are keen to answer. Sometimes we can reformulate the question for the audience, if we think the question is worthwhile. But most times, taking the conversation with the expert audience member to the side after the presentation is over is the best approach.

A very interesting and useful section from *Alexei Kapterev* is given below for FAQs and going through them will help you clear some of your doubts.

Frequently Asked Questions about Delivery- Alexei-Kapterev

Question 1: "I am afraid that I'll forget my speech; can I use my notes or cue cards? Can I read my presentation?"

The short answer is no. I really don't recommend it. Being a big fan of authenticity, I am always suspicious of people who read their notes. However, I can also quote a longer answer from "the TED Commandments," which is the official recommendation for TED speakers: "If your choice is between reading or rambling, then read!"

But if you have slides, you shouldn't be rambling, should you? They do work as cue cards and notes. Well, for some people they do, for some they don't. When death by PowerPoint was at full swing, people were putting text on their slides and reading it aloud, turning their backs to the audience. This was a disaster. This was even worse than reading prepared speeches from paper. But now, there isn't much text on our slides and people are forced to speak from their minds. Honesty, at last! Right? Wrong. People still can't speak from their minds; it's too risky.

What do you do, then? In the best case, you rehearse so vigorously that you end up memorising the words, and sound canned and unnatural. But look, there's another possibility: You can get back to the 20th century and read from your notes, showing your beautiful laconic slides as a nice prop. What a triumph of mind!

Mark Twain once said that if you tell the truth, you don't have to remember anything. If you just talk without notes and make eye contact, your audience will assume that you're honest. Suddenly, you become trustworthy and authentic.

Question 2: "How do I set up a 'confidence monitor'?"

A confidence monitor shows your current slide on the laptop positioned in front of you (so you don't need to turn your back to the audience to look at the screen) and your next slide. So you can confidently move along. It might also display the current time or a countdown timer. The figure below shows a screenshot from *Apple Keynote's presenter screen.*

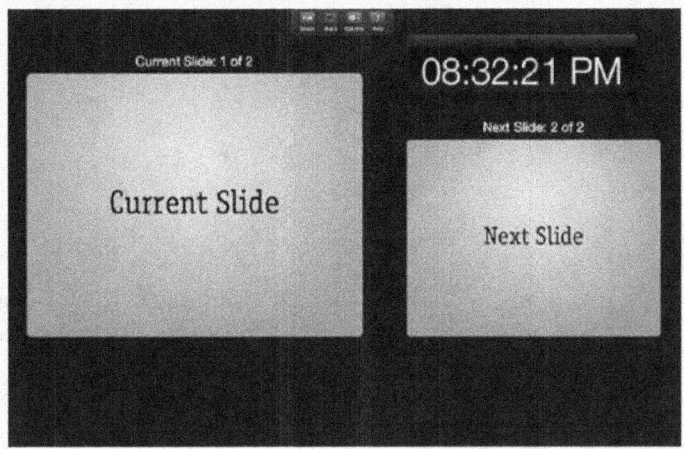

You can also get almost the exact same picture in the PowerPoint. I am surprised that so few people use one because it is extremely helpful and activating it actually not that hard.

If you use Keynote and for some reason are unable to position your laptop, you can see your next slide, and you can set up a confidence monitor on your iPad or iPhone (I'm pretty sure you've got one) using a $1 application from Apple called *Keynote Remote* and a *Wi-Fi connection.*

And here's an even simpler trick that saved me on a number of occasions: When I present at an unfamiliar venue, I carry a 5-metre VGA extension cord. If the projector cord is too short, I can deal with that.

The next figure explains how to do it in PowerPoint and Keynote.

Question 3: "What's with the remote controllers I see some presenters have?"

Get yourself a remote controller. A clicker or A presenter. Call it whatever you want, but do it now. Seriously. I mean it, now. There are lots of infrared controllers; don't buy any of those. They aren't reliable enough. You can never be sure that it will actually turn the next slide after you press the Next button. It doesn't bring you much confidence. Get yourself a radio remote by Logitech, Keyspan, Kensington, or any other reputable company. They are not very expensive, and you'll save much more on anxiety pills. These remotes typically work within a 60–100 feet range with both Macs and PCs and they require no setup.

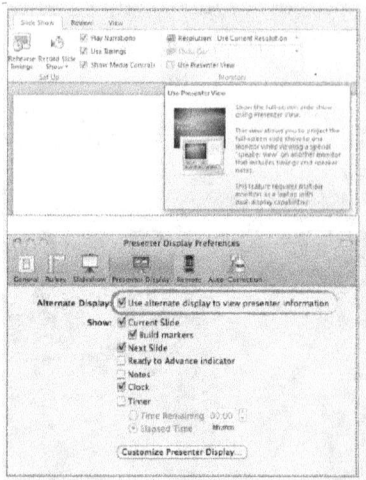

Some advanced models have countdown timers with silent vibration alarms, volume controls, and many other immensely useful features like cool green laser pointers, etc.

Please don't use *radio mice* to control your presentation. They look amateurish, and I mean that in a bad way.

Source: Presentation Secrets by Alexei Kapterev
Recall
Let us recall some salient points regarding delivery:
1. Focus on the Audience
- ✓ Practise your delivery so that you can focus on the audience while you're presenting— don't focus on what to say next. Don't repeat the same words while practising; you will sound canned.
- ✓ Maintain eye contact. Scan the audience from one side to another, making sure you look into the eye of everyone who is in the room.
- ✓ Talk to the people, not just in their general direction.

2. What's the Challenge?
- ✓ Ask questions even if you don't expect an answer. Challenge them. Give them difficult choices.
- ✓ Don't shy away from conflict, embrace it. If nobody's objecting that means you're not saying anything particularly interesting. Fear and resistance to change are perfectly natural. You need to address these concerns.
- ✓ If somebody asks a question, make sure you still talk to the whole audience, not just to one person.

3. Admit Mistakes

- ✓ Switch from censoring to monitoring. Say what you think but listen to what you say.
- ✓ When things go wrong, don't try to hide it. Mistakes create tension, which is best released with laughter.
- ✓ Be your hero. Improvise.

A Case

In August 2010, there was some debate in London whether the Southbank Centre, one of Britain's National Theatre sites, should be listed as a building of historical significance. The debate became particularly heated when Steve Norris, a London Mayoral advisor, gave this comment to the *Evening Standard*: "Not only do I not want the Southbank Centre to be listed—I think the National Theatre should have a Compulsory Demolition Order!"

Apparently, some people at the National Theatre got upset. The theatre had a Twitter account set up for purely PR purposes. As with most accounts set up for PR purposes, it was rather boring and self-aggrandising. I don't know what happened exactly, but their reply to the Standard commentary was surprisingly blunt: "Well, Steve Norris is clearly a giant ****" with asterisks representing one of the most offensive words in English language.

Some 50 minutes later, an apology was issued stating that the account has been compromised and that the tweet did not come from the Theatre staff. We don't know whether the account was really hacked or not, but the point is that nobody believed it. The most popular hypothesis the public formed was that somebody from the PR staff forgot to log off from the official account before tweeting to their personal one. It's an understandable mistake. It's like sending a text message to the wrong person or mistakenly pressing the 'Reply All' button. Everybody does that once or twice, and the reaction from most Twitter users was surprisingly positive:

- ✓ @DisAgg – And to think I'd thought about unfollowing @NationalTheatre for them being bland. Best. Tweet. Ever.
- ✓ @johnfoley – Have to say I found that errant @NationalTheatre tweet to be refreshingly human.
- ✓ @jmc_fire – To be honest, I thought the @nationaltheatre c-word tweet was less offensive than their selective tweeting of good feedback on their shows.
- ✓ @NJMiller – This is the only interesting thing @nationaltheatre has ever tweeted.
- ✓ @LozKaye – For the first time ever I feel tempted to follow @NationalTheatre.

One blogger by the name of Megan Vaughn wrote later: "For a moment there, you were my hero. The previously lacklustre self-promotion that littered your feed was briefly enlivened . . . . You, our National Theatre . . ., were human after all. . . . Hooray for the National Theatre! Hooray for passionate tweets about relevant issues!" Hooray to passionate presentations about relevant issues!

The real mistake here wasn't the tweet. The real mistake was taking it back in such a manner. Instead of simply apologising in a straightforward way and perhaps gaining more credibility, the National Theatre tried to deflect criticism with an excuse that almost no one believed (whether or not it was really true). The reaction of the various Twitter users shows how much more the public valued the reaction, the language that seemed authentic over that which seemed canned and constructed.

Source: Presentation Secrets by Alexei Kapterev

Chapter 8

We introduced visual aids earlier in the book but as it is an independent section, we have a small chapter dedicated to this. Let us discuss various types of visual aids:

1. Text Slide

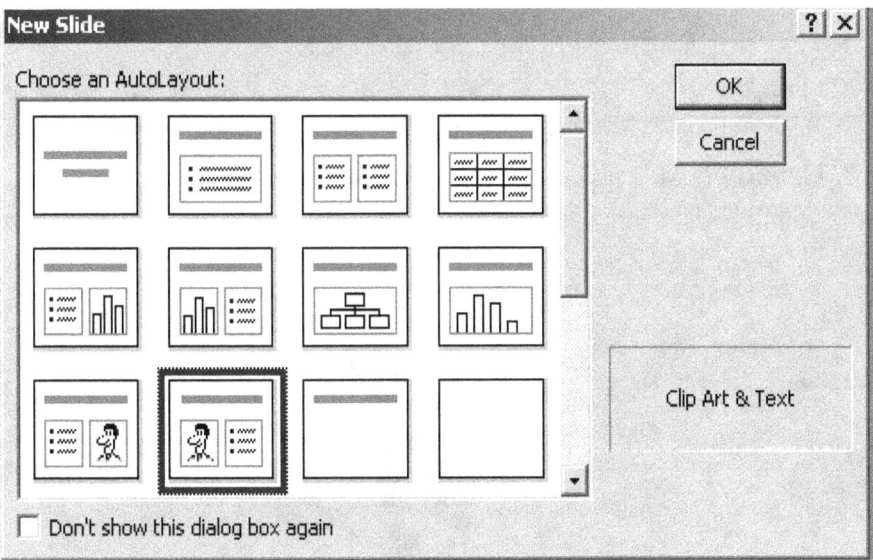

When to use:

On a rare occasion, when you may have a quote, a list of instructions, an agenda or you need to enhance a point that would otherwise be lost.

When not to use:

Try and avoid using text slides wherever possible.

2. High Resolution Images - *Sourced from sites such as Flickr.com*

When to use:

These slides are used typically when you have a large audience. However they may be used quite effectively with smaller groups.

When not to use:

Don't rely solely on this type of slide when conducting business presentations.

3. Prezi:
Prezi is a cloud-based presentation software and storytelling tool for exploring and sharing ideas on a virtual canvas.

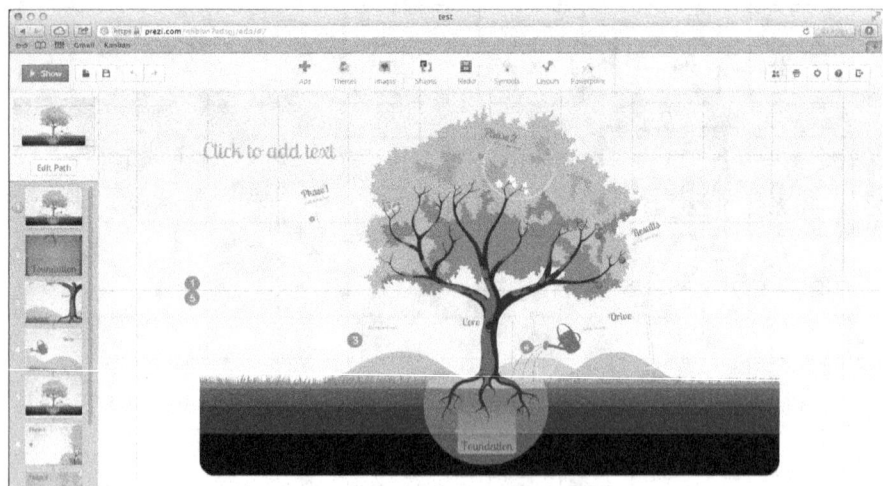

When to use:

When you need to entertain, demonstrate a "fly through" of a concept, or use as a tracking device in workshops, so that people can see where they have been and where they are going.

When not to use:

To replace your normal Powerpoint deck with this tool for the sole reason of making it more interesting.

4. You! - Dressing, grooming and hygiene.

When to use:

Think about your audience and their expectations of you. Even if your audience is informal, there may be an expectation that you dress in a more formal manner.

When not to use:

Don't wear ill-fitting, worn out, inappropriate and out-dated clothing, don't wear accessories with tragic hair, don't forget about grooming and don't wear inappropriate accessories.

5. One Page - Refer *extremepresentation.com* for some ideas on how to do this.

When to use:

When you want people to follow your logic, you can lay all your information out on one page. So it's easy to follow.

When not to use:

Not useful when you have to entertain an audience.

6. Wide Screen TV - A flat panel display of 76 cm or larger.

When to use:

It works well for small meeting rooms. The quality can be better than projectors, particularly when displaying the images or playing videos.

When not to use :

As for other technologies, they are a means for projecting your work. If you haven't worked hard on your content, no technology will make it look better.

7. Flip Charts

When to use:

Very useful for facilitation, try pre-drawing headings and even pencilling in diagrams that can be drawn over.

When not to use:

Not useful for short presentations unless they are pre-drawn and you need to add just a small piece of information.

8. Slide Share - Slide Share is a means of presenting yourself or your business or ideas online.

When to use:

This should only be used for one person to view and read on line. Look at competition winners for slides that follow good design principles.

When not to use:

They should not be projected unless they are there to inform or entertain and conform to the high resolution guidelines by *Duarte* and *Reynolds*, once again references above.

9. Marketing Decks - In order to ensure results, sufficient information is handed onto the sales team, marketing will publish product information in a PPT deck comprising many pages.

When to use:

This should be used as a hand out, reference document or leave behind.

When not to use:

Should never be projected.

10. Video

When to use:

Inserted into a PPT deck, or on their own can be very effective. Useful for quote's or product demonstrations or vox pops.

When not to use:

As a presentation filler, a way to fill in time, the video or audio must be highly relevant.

Here, we come to the end of this small chapter of *various types of visual aids required in a presentation.*

Chapter 9

The following chapter gives 26 tips to make and deliver a good presentation. Keep these tips handy and master the skill of an effective presentation.

Audience:

When preparing to meet your audience, remember never to overestimate their knowledge or underestimate their intelligence.

There are a Number of Questions to Consider When You Begin to Plan Your Presentation:

Who is going to be there?

Who are my "friends/well-wishers" and who are my "enemies"?

How can I use my friends before the presentation?

What can I do to change the mindset of my enemies before the presentation (through phone calls, emails, pre-presentation meetings, etc.)

How much do they know about my subject?

How much do I know about them?

✓ What are their expectations?
✓ Is someone going to introduce me – if so, what will they say?
✓ What issues/difficult questions am I likely to encounter?

Backward Planning:

The best place to start thinking about your presentation is the end! Start with the end objectives in mind and plan backwards how to achieve them.

Following are the Three Techniques to Help You with this:

Write down on a piece of paper, "After my presentation, the audience will be able to………." Now complete the sentence. This will give you a good feel of what you expect the audience to do/say after your presentation. Ask yourself, "What is the most important thing here – if I wanted to convince my audience of only one thing, what would that be?"

Write the last slide first. This will encourage you to think of your ending, and picture the outcome you want as you start to hear the applause from the audience.

Imagine that a journalist is going to do a write-up in the newspaper the day after your presentation – what would you want him/her to write? "Navneet Mehra secures the biggest order in the company's history!" or "Navneet Mehra gives them a lot to think about!" etc.

As a result of your backward planning, you will be able to draw up a plan for *delivering*, *preparing* and *writing* your presentation.

Content:

Before your presentation, write down any facts and ideas, you can think of. Imagine that you are going to deliver a customer presentation featuring a new product. When planning the presentation, the above three categories might look like this................

Things they must know	Things they should know	Things they could know
Why the product was introduced	How the product has benefited customers similar to them	The detailed story behind the research and product development
The features of the new product and how it compares to other products on the market		Press comments
The benefits of the new product – i.e. the value it will add to the customer's business		

Give your 'must know' factors plenty of space so that they don't get lost in a lot.

Different Room Layouts:

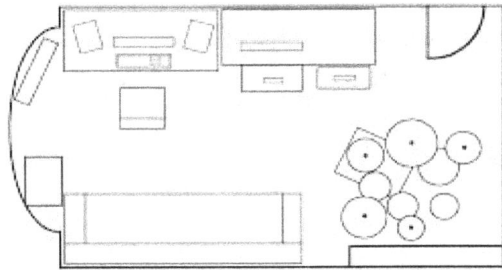

The best room layout is the one you want to use, not necessarily the one you are presented with. Though there is also a golden rule here – Don't use the layout you are presented with, try and influence the layout to create the environment you want.

Equipments:

A-Z of Presentation Skills

When using visual equipment, there are some 'do's and don'ts' that are worth mentioning:

For Powerpoint Projector:
- ✓ Avoid too many slides
- ✓ Don't repeat every word on the screen
- ✓ Use pictures/graphs
- ✓ No more than one slide per minute
- ✓ Use 36-40pt as a minimum

For Overhead Projector:
- ✓ Locate OHP at desk height
- ✓ Put slides on machine before you switch it on
- ✓ Make sure the full OHP picture is on the screen
- ✓ Don't look at the screen – use a pen as a pointer on top of the projector

Remember: Always have 'Plan B' ready. If your projector breaks, be prepared to carry on and issue handouts.

Flying Starts:

Presentations are like aeroplanes. They are at their most dangerous level when they take off or land! *The first, and last two minutes in a presentation are crucial.*

Gestures:

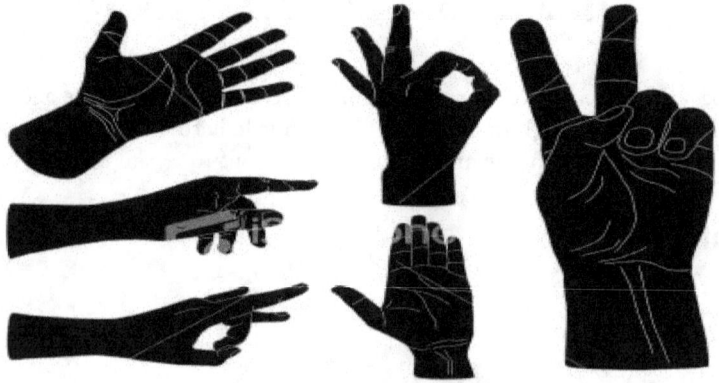

Most audiences like to see the presenter moving around from time to time using hand gestures to illustrate a point. Remember to smile and engage with peoples' eyes – it will relax the audience, give them confidence in you and suggest that they are about to listen to something enjoyable.

Hiccups:

There will always be the occasional hiccup, as things which are out of your control will happen during your presentation. For example a fire alarm may go off, someone might enter the room with a message for one of the members among the audience or a mobile phone may ring. Here, simply though you can jump in and say, "Not to worry, as I was saying……………." but try doing it the other way. Look a little lost and say, "Where was I?". Now the group will have to do the work, as they will get away from the distraction and try to be focussed to the last topic being presented.

Hygiene Factor:

These are things which will not matter if they are right but will surely matter and de-motivate the people if they are wrong. For example, the temperature of the room or the lighting or the ventilation, etc. comes under 'hygiene factors'.

Involvement:

If you want people to get involved in your presentation and participate, first point is to remember to tell them. In many cases, the presenter forgets to tell them that he/she wanted them to be active and ask questions.

Jokes and Humour:

We all know the value of using humour during our work. But when you are presenting to a group of people, however, there are few guidelines:

Don't use humour if it is not your natural style. Don't tell people you are about to tell them a funny story (because they won't find it that funny – it will fall well short of their expectations).

Make sure that the humour is linked to the presentation in some way, else it will confuse people and they will find it difficult to see its relevance.

Keywords or Scripts:

Should you use keywords or should you write the presentation completely and use a script? There is always a healthy debate on this subject, although if had to choose one, the winner would be the 'keywords'. Keywords act as a natural prompt and encourage the presenter to use a relaxed, warm conversational style which is not the case in scripts.

Listening:

Presenters concentrate on giving information rather than receiving it. However, if involvement and questions from the audience are required, *listening is a key skill for a presenter.*

Meetings:

Meetings have a bad name in the industry. If we be to the point, by meeting, one thinks it as a boring activity or a lecture or a timepass, away from regular work. However, meetings do have a number of benefits over other forms of communication: They save us time – something important can be communicated to a group of people much quicker than one-to-one basis.

They provide an ideal problem-solving environment.

Good meetings can be very motivational, as they provide an opportunity for recognition and praise.

Meetings are an excellent teambuilding opportunity. They allow groups of disparate individuals to work together towards common goals.

Narrative:

During your presentation, try and tell stories from time to time. People find them interesting and enjoyable.

Objections:

If you face a number of objections during your presentation, remember the "Three-What" technique. There are three key questions beginning with "what?" followed by "what else?" then "what if?" Let us see an example to understand this.

Example:

Navneet (a Customer in the audience): "I'm not sure about this as it all sounds rather expensive".

You: What exactly do you mean Navneet?

Navneet: Well, it is a good 25% over our budget!!

You: What Else is Holding You up – Is there Anything Else I Need to Know?

Navneet: Yes, there is actually. We need some reassurance that your company can handle a piece of business this size.

You: So what if I was able to look at our price and bring it closer to your budget and also get you in touch with some of our customers who have used us recentl.y would you be happy to go ahead?

Navneet: Yes

Pitch, Pace and Pauses:

Try to pitch your voice up one level from normal. Slow down your pace when you are about to cover the most important points. *Also, don't forget the power of silence.* After you have presented a key point that you want your audience to think about or reflect on, try pausing for 3-4 seconds before moving on.

Questions:

Questions from your audience are actually a good sign – they suggest that people are 'with you' and are showing an interest, that's why they have come up with questions.

are asked:

The question they can't answer. In this case, don't bluff your answer, offer to come back with the answer later.

The relevant question which has already been covered. In that case, thank the questioner (as the question is relevant) and give a quick recap.

The relevant question which has not yet covered. In that case, thank the questioner but point out that you are only a few minutes away from answering the point.

The irrelevant harmless question. In that case, rather than saying that the question is irrelevant, ask, "Navneet, I'm struggling a little with the relevance of that point, could you explain what's behind your question?" Now the questioner will probably see that the question is irrelevant and accept your offer to discuss it later on.

✓ The irrelevant harmful question. In this case, slowdown, buy more time by asking for more information. You may like to use peer group pressure by appealing to the rest of the audience by asking, "What does everyone else think of Gaurav's question?"

Return Visits:

Sometimes, you might make a second visit to present your solutions to a customer and there will be people who were not there in the first meeting. This list will be useful:Introduce yourself to the new entries.

✓ Ask how much they know about the first meeting

✓ Recap as necessary about the first meeting.

✓ Explain your objectives for the second meeting

✓ Check the time available and any likely interruptions to your presentation

✓ Pre-close to check interest and commitment. 'If you like my presentation today and agree that it meets your needs where do we go from here? What would the next stage be?'

Slides:

Keep the following points in mind when designing your slides:

Slides that show *diagrams, charts, graphs, cartoons,* etc are more interesting than row after row of words. Keep the slides simple – one slide should convey only one idea. Do not print anything vertically – it will be too difficult to read. Have no more than 3-4 lines of bullet-point text.

Use colours well, i.e., red for danger/problems/issues, green for strengths/solutions/answers.

Team Briefing:

Team briefings tend to be short, sharp, informative and motivational. As information passes through an organisation, a template is often needed to ensure that people receive the same information at the same time in the same way.

Understanding Body Language Signals:

It is quite a bulky topic to discuss here, but there are few general body language techniques which represent/give some information:

SIGNAL	PROBABLE MEANING
Furrowed forehead	Negative thoughts or concentration
Tapping foot	Impatience, irritation
Avoiding eye contact	Anxiety, suspicion, confusion, shyness
Scratching, pinching or pressing	Punishing self or wants to punish another
Clenching fists	Holding back anger
Finger jabbing	Criticism
Arms folded, legs crossed	Putting up defence barriers
Hand covering mouth	Hiding, playing games, yawning
Physical stroking of face	Comforting self
Intense eye contact	Anger or concern

If, during your presentation, you detect someone in the audience looking confused, upset or angry, don't ignore them. You could deal with the problem there and then by saying, "Bunny, you look a little confused……."

Visual Aids:

These are excellent for changing the senses during your presentation, but if you are going to use visual aids, there are number of guidelines:

Keep it/them out of sight until needed, otherwise they will become a distraction. Remove it after you have used it, otherwise it will (again) become a distraction.

Written Proposals:

If you are presenting to customers or prospects, they will often expect a written proposal. *Written proposals make customers feel reassured.*

Here are the Main Points to Remember, if you are Going to Use a Written Proposal to Support Your Presentation:

Invest the time needed to create the right impression. Think about using customer logos (with their permission) on the front cover and a theme that the customer will relate to.

✓ Make sure that names and titles are correct – Navneet Mehra, Technical Director will not react favourably to being called Navneet Mehra, Director of Technologies.

✓ Use colour, graphs, charts and other interesting visuals

✓ Date the proposal and number the pages

Write It as You would Say It, i.e., Spoken English not

Written English	Spoken English
I am in receipt of	Thanks for
In regard to	About
The undersigned	We
Will you be so kind as to	Could you
In the event that	If
As per our agreement	As agreed
In the normal course of events	Usually
At the present time of writing	Today
At a later date	Later
I want to say that it was a pleasure	I enjoyed
I myself personally	I

A-Z of Presentation Skills

X-Tra Things to Do Later:

Pack up your kit and leave the venue looking clean and tidy.

Remove any handouts (you don't want them falling into the hands of your competitors) and any confidential flip chart pages.

CRITERIA	10% FOR EACH IF PRESENT
1. Did I present to all of the decision makers and influencers?	
2. Did I identify the needs accurately?	
3. Was my presentation tailored to meet those needs?	
4. Were any objections or problems openly discussed?	
5. Is their decision-making process free from company politics?	
6. Is our price right?	
7. Have we got the ability and experience to deliver the solution?	
8. Have we got the upper hand over our competitors?	
9. Have I effectively explained benefits v costs?	
10. Are they making the right positive noises towards us?	
TOTAL OUT OF 100	? %

Let us assume, you have just delivered a presentation to a customer you may want to reflect on the % probability of the business coming your way. Ask yourself "What is the % probability now and what do I have to do to make it 100% probable?" The checklist below can be quite useful. (Change the numbers, if you feel that the scores should be weighted.)

Send an email to thank the organiser, the IT person who helped with your slides or anyone who deserves a thanks.

Your Ongoing Development:

A brief A-Z chapter cannot turn you into a brilliant speaker – only practice can do that. Don't wait for months to go by before you deliver another presentation – push yourself to keep doing them at every available opportunity.

Zero-Ten Evaluation:

Get some critical feedback on your presentation. Ask people to comment on your content, your style, the duration, the quality of any materials used, the way that you handled questions from the audience, the interest level, etc. Don't forget to ask about the joining instructions, venue and facilities if under your control. Talk to people face to face or use an evaluation form to ask them:

✓ "What was the most useful aspect of my presentation?"
✓ "What was the least useful aspect?"
✓ "How many marks out of ten would you give it?"
✓ "What would I have to do to score ten?"
✓ "How could my presentation have been improved?"

If you worked with a colleague during the presentation, ask for feedback on your contribution and then give your feedback on theirs.

SELF-IMPROVEMENT/PERSONALITY DEVELOPMENT

Also Available in Kannada

Also Available in Kannada

      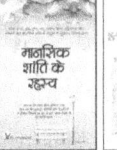 

All books available at www.vspublishers.com

QUIZ BOOKS

ENGLISH IMPROVEMENT

CTIVITIES BOOK | QUOTES/SAYINGS

BIOGRAPHIES

IELTS TECH

CHILDREN SCIENCE LIBRARY

COMPUTER BOOKS

Also available in Hindi   Also available in Hindi

All books available at www.vspublishers.com

STUDENT DEVELOPMENT/LEARNING

POPULAR SCIENCE

Also Available in Hindi

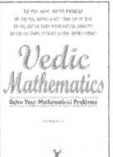

Also Available in Hindi   Also Available in Hindi

PUZZLES

Also Available in Hindi   Also Available in Hindi

DRAWING BOOKS

Also Available in Hindi   Also Available in Hindi, Tamil & Bangla

REGIONAL LANGUAGE   OTHER BOOKS

(Telugu)   (Odia)   (Marathi)   (Bangla)

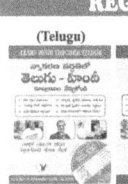

Also Available in Hindi   Also Available in Hindi   Also Available in Hindi

CHILDREN'S ENCYCLOPEDIA – THE WORLD OF KNOWLEDGE

Contact us at sales@vspublishers.com

www.ingramcontent.com/pod-product-compliance
Lightning Source LLC
Chambersburg PA
CBHW070335230426
43663CB00011B/2326